A Review of Books, Studies and Journal Articles Published in the U.S.A. from 1955-1995 Relating to the Sociological Impact of Corporate Relocation on the Family System

by

Barbara W. Cummings, Ph.D.

ISBN: 1-58112-053-2

DISSERTATION.COM

1999

ISBN: 1-58112-053-2

Published by
Dissertation.com
USA
1999

www.dissertation.com/library/1120532a.htm

A REVIEW OF BOOKS, STUDIES AND JOURNAL ARTICLES PUBLISHED IN THE U.S.A. FROM 1955-1995 RELATING TO THE SOCIOLOGICAL IMPACT OF CORPORATE RELOCATION ON THE FAMILY SYSTEM

Barbara W. Cummings, B.S., M.A.

A Dissertation Presented to the Faculty of the Graduate School of Saint Louis University in Partial Fulfillment of the Requirements for the Degree of Doctor of Philosophy

1998

1998

COMMITTEE IN CHARGE OF CANDIDACY:

Professor Emeritus Albert "Rick" Bender,
Chairperson and Advisor

Professor Michael P. Grady

Assistant Professor Dorothy D. Miles

ACKNOWLEDGEMENTS

I would like to acknowledge and thank Professor Rick Bender who not only chaired the committee but also was a helpful mentor to me throughout the process. In addition, I would like to thank the other members of my committee Professor Michael Grady and Assistant Professor Dorothy Miles for their academic guidance and support. To Dr. Gerald Fowler, whose kind words encouraged me to pursue my Ph.D. and to Michael Garanzini S.J., a brilliant teacher and my first advisor, whose help and assistance I can never repay.

I would like to acknowledge my husband Michael. This dissertation could not have been completed without his love and never ending support. And, to my children, Tracy and Sean who survived a rootless childhood to become strong adults whom I respect and admire.

To all, my deepest gratitude and love.

TABLE OF CONTENTS

LIST OF TABLES

LIST OF FIGURES

CHAPTER I

INTRODUCTION

Statement of the Problem

While the "mobility of peoples is a historic and universal phenomenon as certain as death and taxes" (Sussman & Settles, 1993, p. 213), America is a mobile nation even by world standards. The average American moves 14 times, while in Great Britain the number is eight, in Japan five, and France seven, (Glueck, 1974; Long, 1970; Packard, 1972).

According to the latest census report, one in five Americans moves each year for an average of forty-three million Americans changing residences (Hansen, U.S. Bureau of Census, 1996). It is estimated that of these, "twenty-two million made moves that were job related" (Ammons, Nelson, & Wodarski, 1982, p. 207; Gaylord & Symons, 1986, p. 31).

Corporate relocation has become a way of life for many executives and their families who frequently move every two to three years (Anderson & Stark, 1985; Bayes, 1989). Porter and Rand said, "one of the interesting things about this phenomenon is that while we are moving a great deal, it is not something that we do easily or without pain"(1992, p. 7). In addition, according to Anderson and Stark (1988, p. 38),

> relocating families have been found to share a common array of stresses, including loss of support networks and valued persons and things (such as friendship groups or the family home); acquisition of greater role burdens (a traditional example would be the wife covering for the husband while he moved ahead to a

> new job); and interruption of personal growth and development (a teenager might forfeit autonomy when forced to leave a part-time job).

Friedman believes that this mobility "has profound and often negative consequences for the spouse, the marriage, children and the family" (1989, p. 1).

Brief Review of Related Literature

One of the earliest mobility researchers was Peter Rossi who wrote Why Families Move in 1955. His book examined the forces at work in the decision making process of relocating families. By the sixties, corporate transfers accounted for 296,000 relocations annually (Sell, 1982). By the mid seventies, that number was estimated at 750,000 and executives at IBM joked that the initials stood for "I've Been Moved" (Loomis, 1992, p. 7).

Transfers became accepted as a routine part of corporate life. Vance Packard's A Nation of Strangers in 1972 and Robert Seidenberg's Corporate Wives–Corporate Casualties the following year both hit a collective nerve, but mobility statistics were rising. Sociologists often refer to the seventies as the beginning of *the me generation.* With priorities focused on material gain, this generation was emotionally well equipped for climbing the corporate ladder relocation by relocation. Apparently, little thought was being given to whether competitive individualistic values were healthy for themselves or their families. Some felt,

> . . . repeated uprooting tends to reinforce a materialistic orientation to life, because as the family is perpetually having to present an image to strangers and getting fewer rewards from emotional connections, issues of status and appearance come to dominate. In turn, the materialistic, rather than relational, striving reinforces mobility, which again reinforces materialism, and we get caught in an American vicious circle. (Nicols & Schwartz, 1991, p. 92)

Not all researchers even agree that relocation is stressful. Landis and Stoetger (1966) and Glueck (1974) reported no apparent related stress among families. Another conflict arises between Edstrom and Galbraith (1977) and Pinder (1979). Edstrom and Galbraith report transfers serve to reinforce one's commitment to one's company and Pinder reports that transfers have the opposite effect.

More recent studies have focused on dual-career issues. Brett and Werbel reported in 1980 that a wife's involvement in her work was a factor in her willingness to relocate. At the time "the sample of mobile working wives was quite small, and less than 50% of these women were working full time" (Brett, 1982, p. 461). Current studies indicate that 55% of all couples relocating have both husband and wife working. It is predicted that by the year 2000 it will be 63% (Brett, Stroh, & Reilly, 1990). This is one of several trends to be examined in the review.

There appear to be a great number of books, studies, and research articles dealing with corporate relocation. Each seems to have its own particular focus or approach such as: Relocation following divorce; self-esteem of the trailing spouse; dual-career couples; developing social networks following relocation; residential change and school adjustment; geographic relocation and extended family cohesion; residential mobility as an adaptive experience; mothers' anxieties versus the effects of long distance moves on children; to name only a few. Each looks at part of the relocation picture, but not the picture as a whole.

Theoretical Framework – Family Systems Theory

A systems perspective says that each of our interactions affects the other and, in part, we become responsible for another's actions because our actions have in part affected their reaction (Becvar & Becvar, 1982).

An individual perspective would say – A causes B.

Figure 1. - Linear cause-effect

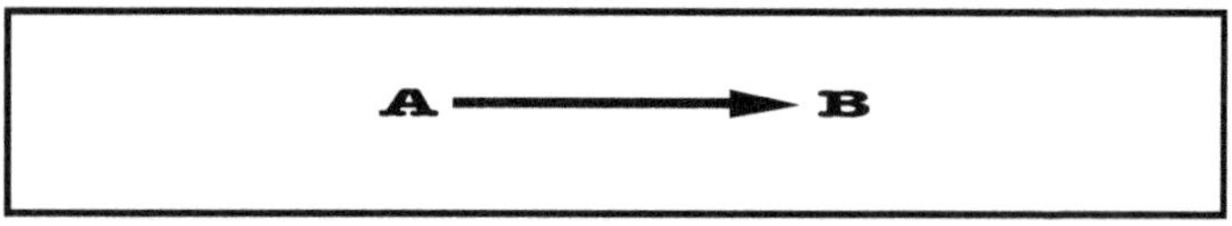

A systems perspective would say – There is a reciprocal dynamic interaction between A and B.

Figure 2. - Reciprocal cause-effect

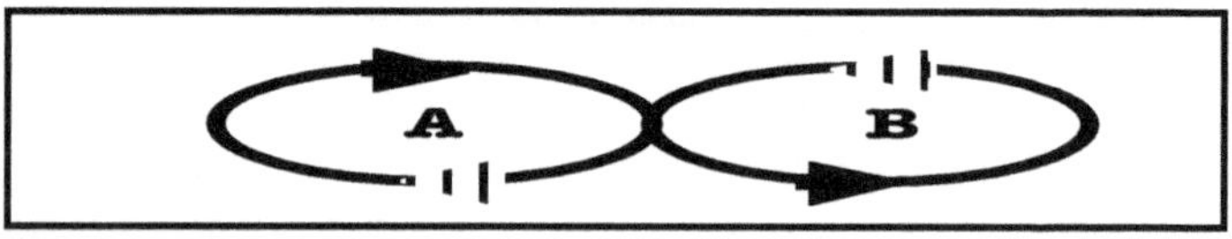

According to Carter and McGoldrick, "families can be seen as a network of interlocking triangles in which each member is close to some and distant from others in a complicated web of alliances and tensions" (1989, p. 204). The more members in the family, the more complex the interaction. The Becvars believe that in a nuclear family of two parents and two children there are four triangles (see Figure 3 - Example 1). If you increase this by just one other child the triangles increase to 10 (see Figure 3 - Example 2). The Becvars add even more triangles because they say a family of five has five persons but ten relationships and 27 triangles for a total of 42 units. They say that the whole is greater than the sum of its parts, or one plus one equals three, for two people relating to each other are not independent but interact with each other forming an extra unit. Therefore, if one considers larger families, the complexity of the relationships multiplies rapidly as shown by the six-person group (see Figure 3 - Example 3).

Figure 3. - Illustration of Bossard's law of family interaction

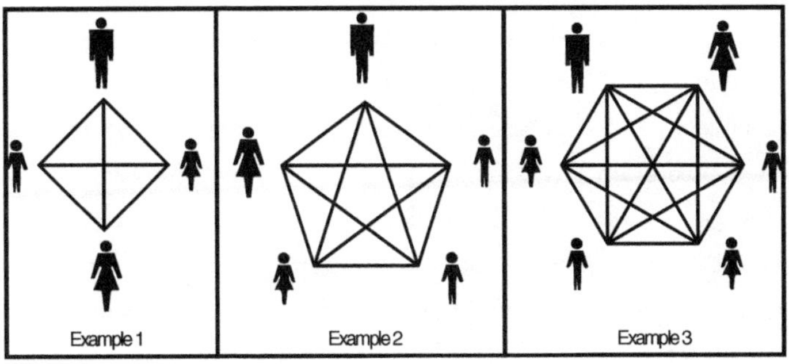

Bossard pointed out that "an arithmetic increase or decrease in the number of members in a primary group is accompanied by a corresponding geometric increase or decrease in the number of relationships in that group" (Bossard, 1945, p. 293). When a geographic relocation is viewed from a systems perspective we can see how it affects everyone in the system. The more members in the family, the more complex the interaction.

Boundaries serve to protect systems from outside forces and help maintain the integrity of its subsystems. How easily systems boundaries are crossed differentiate a system as open or closed. Open systems interact with the outside environment. Closed systems do not. Closed family systems that hold on to the traditions of the past and avoid change are in danger of becoming rigid and isolated. Most experts seem to agree that a healthy system is one that has the ability to adapt and change. In a healthy family system morphogenesis (change) and morphostasis (stability) are both necessary, and an extreme in either would be considered dysfunctional.

In a relocation many changes are taking place for family members who may experience these changes as losses in their life. Not only are there residence and job changes, there are often relationship, school, and social network changes as well. These changes may be enough to cause an overload or pile-up of stress on the family, especially if family members perceive them as losses. Kaplan (1983) believed that it was the unscheduled life events, especially those involving loss, that caused the most stress. In addition, when the stress was experienced by an individual, because of the interrelated roles, it affected the entire family system.

In times of stress the tendency is for the family system to close in order to protect itself. This may result in behavior changes for family members, who after repeated uprooting, may be so enmeshed in a closed family system that they are no longer able to develop close friendships outside the family. This may leave the family less well equipped to deal with family crises at times when outside support is needed and no close friends or extended family members are available.

Relocation and Stress

Almost all researchers agree that a relocation involves considerable stress for the family including Ammons et al. (1982), Anderson and Stark (1988), Bayes (1989), Gullotta and Donohue (1981), Jennings (1967), McCollum (1990), Weiss (1973), and Weissman and Paykel (1972).

Renshaw believed that stress is actually composed of two distinct and separate elements, the objective properties of the event and the subjective meaning that the event holds for the individual (1976, p. 164). The amount of *felt* stress is directly related to how stressful the individual perceives the stressor to be. "Stress in one system is not caused by events in the other system, but is a function of the interactive nature of the relationship of the two systems" (ibid.).

McCubbin and Patterson (1983a) said the family's perception of the event as stressful or not was an essential element in the family's ability to cope. Stress might never reach crisis proportions if the family did not perceive an event as stressful. However, they said that it was possible for a pile-up of changes to occur which would then exhaust the family's ability to cope and leave the family vulnerable to a crisis.

Kantor (1963) also believed that the number of stressors was significant and Anderson and Stark (1988) said that the number and frequency of relocations was significant in how the family coped with the current relocation. In another study by Loomis (1992), those families who had *difficult* moves had experienced twice the number of concurrent transitions.

Another factor influencing how the family experiences the move is whether the move is voluntary or involuntary. Renshaw (1976) believed that the greater the amount of control, or choice one had regarding the relocation, the less negative the experience would be. Renshaw added that the impact of the move "is systemic, as it involves both the work and the family system and the effects are apparent eventually in both systems" (p. 154). Feitler-Karchin and Getting agreed, saying that "moving was one of the most stressful events that can occur in one's life, particularly if the relocation is one that has not been made by positive personal choice" (1987, p. 59). Loomis believed that if one had no control over the relocation process, one was vulnerable to "anger and negative consequences" (1992, p. 34).

Relocation and Loss

Constable said, "a move is something like a death; a part of us dies, is separated, we mourn and we experience grief and loss" (1978, p. 419). Gaylord stated that psychoanalytic literature had dealt with the consequences of separation and loss for decades, but it was only in recent years that "the literature dealt with geographic moves and their potential detrimental effects on the individual or family" (1979, p. 186).

According to Starker (1988) and Mettelman (1993) a relocation involves many losses, including loss of friends, community, and familiar routines; it may involve giving up a job, volunteer work, schools and even sometimes the loss of family members who are left behind. Because relocation involves so many losses researchers have found parallels between the relocation process and the grief process.

Jones (1984), Loomis (1992), and Weissman and Paykel (1972) are among those who began referring to Elisabeth Kübler-Ross' *Stages of Death and Dying* when discussing relocation. Dr. Kübler-Ross first published On Death and Dying in 1970 after working with terminally ill patients. It was a new way of looking at grief as a series of stages that one progresses through. It is now in common use by psychologists when working with clients who have experienced traumatic events (Harrison & Rich, 1984).

Stages of Relocation/Kübler-Ross

Stage One: Denial. A patient might refuse to discuss their illness or refuse medication saying they were not ill so they did not need medication.

In relocation a homeowner might refuse to put their house on the market to sell or family members might make long-term commitments in the community that they would not be able to keep.

Denial is the way that one protects oneself from hurt and pain. When denial can no longer be maintained it is replaced with:

Stage Two: Anger. Kübler-Ross said that this was the most difficult stage for the patient and staff as patients vent their anger and frustration.

In relocation, family members also might attack, blame, and criticize the family member or company responsible for the move.

The situation often feels out of control at this stage. When one attempts to regain control one begins moving into the next stage:

Stage Three: Bargaining. A patient might try to bargain with the Doctor for medication or a procedure in order to gain time to visit family or schedule a special holiday. On the other hand, if one is religious, one might make a promise to their god in exchange for time.

In relocation, a spouse might ask for some concession as reward for going or teens might agree to go only if they are allowed to visit their friends the following summer.

When the reality of the situation is faced and the losses that one is about to experience are realized one may experience the next stage:

Stage Four: Depression. In both grief and relocation, it is during this stage that one sees oneself as a victim; one generally rejects offers of help and is unable to envision any possibility of a positive outcome. A feeling of hopelessness and helplessness often accompany this stage. What is needed at this stage is to acknowledge the sense of loss. One must go through the pain of acknowledging the losses before healing can take place.

Stage Five: Acceptance. In both grief and relocation if one has had enough time to go through the stages, then hopefully one arrives at the final stage, which is acceptance.

This stage is often misinterpreted. When one hears the word *acceptance*, one may think that they have not arrived at this stage until they feel happy about the situation. What this stage actually means, according to Kübler-Ross (1970), is that one has finally incorporated this new and perhaps painful situation into their view of reality. When one begins asking for suggestions and ideas, and becomes interested in exploring some of the options open to them, they are considered to have arrived at this stage.

Having now listed the stages, it should immediately be said that one rarely goes through these stages in a neat orderly way. The strong emotions evoked by a serious change in one's life are rarely expressed in a calm orderly way. Each member of a family may feel differently about a move and what seems like an opportunity for one may feel like an unbearable loss for another. One member may rush to acceptance in a matter of days; another may regress back to an earlier stage before moving ahead; and yet another may become *stuck* in a stage, unable move forward. Most researchers believe that as with the grief stages a relocation may take almost two years of adjustment time as shown in Figure 4.

Figure 4. - The stages of relocation (Herring, 1988b)

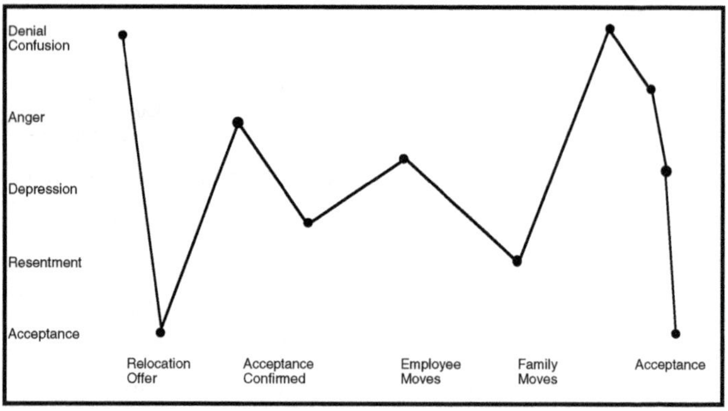

used

Marshall and Cooper described it well when they said that relocation is not simply moving from one geographic area to another, "in between is a fluid, disrupted period of belonging to neither world" (1976, p. 219). For some this can be a few weeks or months and for others this period of not belonging may be as long as two years.

We use the term jet-lag to describe the feelings of being out-of-sync with time when we travel. This process might be thought of as *Relo-Lag*™ [1], for during this time we are not only out-of-sync with our family, but our surroundings as well.

From a systems viewpoint, during a relocation the family system is reorganizing. Within the family system the ability of its members to communicate is vital and defines the nature of the relationships within the family. When family members are at different stages in the relocation process communication is difficult and there may be movement towards "entropy, a disorganized state characterized by a gradual but decreasing level of interaction between members" (Becvar & Becvar, 1982, p. 13). In order to reorganize the family system must find the opposing energy source called negentrophy which "drives systems toward increased patterning, order, and organization" (Robbins, 1992, p. 27).

Relocation is a complex process and there are many factors that contribute to how the family perceives and experiences the relocation.

[1] Relo-Lag is a Trademark of Barbara W. Cummings, 1998. All rights reserved.

Definition of Terms

Sociological Impact: An effect felt by members of a family or larger system, e.g. – Stress symptoms expressed by members of the transferring family often accompany their relocation. Symptoms include (but may not be limited to) depression, deterioration of health, community withdrawal, excessive dependency on the marital relationship for emotional satisfaction, alcoholism, social anonymity, and marital discord and divorce (Anderson & Stark, 1988).

Corporate Relocation: Corporate Relocation is defined by Sekaran as "a change in residence by a salaried employee upon request of corporate management designed to align individual career objectives with the goals of the organization" (1986, in Todd, 1994, p. 3).

Family System: Family System may best be described as a perspective; a way of viewing the family as a whole. One does not focus on the individuals but on the interaction taking place between members and within the family. It is the context of the relationships and their dynamic interaction that is viewed as a whole.

Purpose of Review and Research Questions

While there has been a great deal of research done on corporate relocation, it has mainly addressed specific and limited questions. It was primarily from the perspective of the individual, not the family, and often yielded conflicting results. The purpose of the study is to provide a more cohesive body of work on the sociological impact of relocation on the family system.

The specific questions generated by the purpose of this study were:

1. Does relocation affect the family system? If so, does it involve the interaction only within the family, or larger societal systems as well?
2. If there are effects, what is the nature of the effects and are they short-term, long-term, or both?

In attempting to answer these questions, the review may assist both families and corporations in making more informed and educated decisions regarding relocation.

CHAPTER II

METHODOLOGY

Blessed are the poor in choices, for they will have no trouble making up their minds [1]

Research Approach

After considering the many research options, a qualitative approach is best for this dissertation. The qualitative approach strives to understand the gestalt, the totality of a problem as a whole. This is congruent with the goal of understanding the whole picture of corporate relocation and its impact on the family system. Implicit in this approach is that the picture emerges as the pieces are put together, rather than determined a priori. To illustrate where this type of research fits into the entire body of qualitative research the analogy of a shade tree is shown and described by Harry F. Wolcott in LeCompte, Millroy and Preissle's Qualitative Research in Education (1992, p. 23).

As shown on Figure 5, within the qualitative research area is a branch referred to as "Archival" and on this branch would be "Historical/Document Review" which is the plan for the dissertation.

According to Borg and Gall "historical research is a systematic search for facts relating to questions about the past and the interpretation of these facts" (1989, p. 806).

[1] Halcolm's Evaluation Beatitudes, Patton, 1980, p.17.

They consider historical investigation "part of qualitative research tradition in education" (ibid.).

Figure 5. - Qualitative Strategies in Educational Research

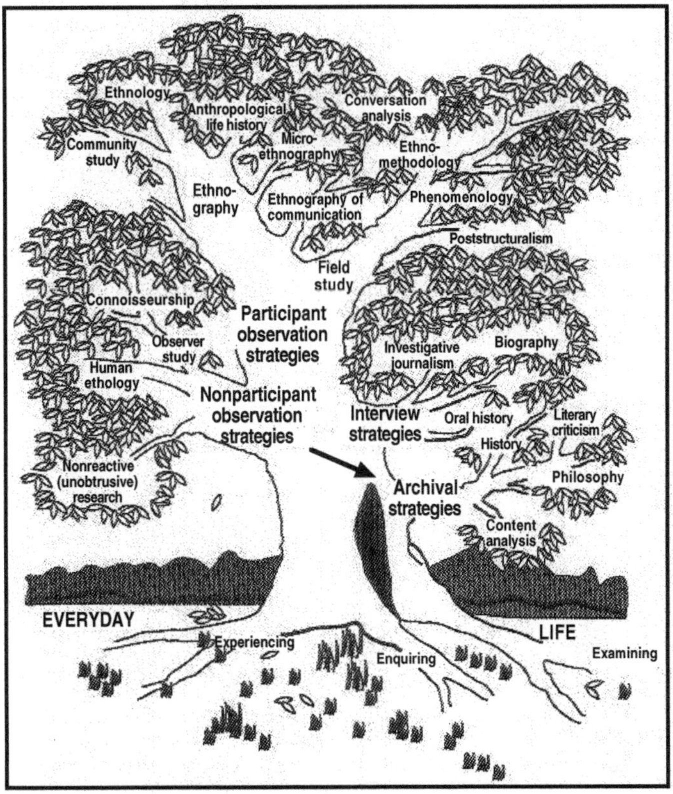

One begins with the early research placing it in its societal context and looks to compare and contrast the literature looking for patterns and trends. Decade by decade to the present the research is evaluated to see where it fits into the emerging picture. The literature is not chosen at random but carefully selected after meeting certain criteria. The basis for selection for the purpose of this dissertation is that it be a book, study, or journal article dealing with the effects of corporate relocation on the family. Research dealing with other aspects of corporate relocation (factory and equipment moves, etc.) would be rejected.

The *tree* entices one to go out on a limb for a better look, and the climb along the way involves making choices and selecting what material *fits*, which, in turn, adds pieces to the picture. The search itself is interesting for the term "relocation" includes everything from corporate to World War II internment camps, moving factory facilities, migration of peoples during famine, and migrant workers. Some writers believe that immigration and corporate mobility are connected. Mobility, moving, move, and adjustment are used interchangeably with relocation. One searches all variations so as not to overlook something relevant, but the focus remains on *corporate relocation*, its history, and how it may have affected American families. Material is available in education, business, psychology, social work, medical, and counseling journals. One should consider all areas as potential sources in gathering material to insure a more complete picture. According to Soltis:

> Education is, at base, a moral enterprise. It is about the formation of persons and developing and contributing to the good life of individuals and society. Even though we may disagree

> about the specifics of what constitutes the educated person and the good life it is toward these high moral ends that the human enterprise of education in a democratic society is negotiated and directed. Research is part of the continuing process of education, it is about contributing to individuals and society. (1990, p. 248)

In the same chapter Soltis declares the qualitative approach is not only best suited to document and understand change, but the effects of change on human beings. A relocation not only involves the physical external change of place for a family, but an internal process of change as well. The topic and the approach are congruent.

CHAPTER III

THE ROOTS OF AMERICAN MOBILITY

***From the earliest pilgrim landings,
through the great westward migrations,
moving and opportunity have been
intertwined in U.S. history*** [1]

Moving for Americans is equated with opportunity and adventure. Some researchers believe that mobility is part of the American culture. They say that as a nation of immigrants, Americans are descendants of those willing to move for opportunity. That, in fact, those who moved perceived this moving as an opportunity when other family members who stayed behind saw only danger ahead (Ramey & Cloud, 1987; Veiga, 1981). According to Duhl (1963), Justice Douglas used the Chinese character for change to illustrate this duality.

Figure 6. - Chinese character for change

The character, according to Justice Douglas can mean either opportunity or danger depending on one's interpretation. Some focus on and see opportunity while others focus on and see only danger. While there are added

[1] McCollum, Jensen, & Copans, 1995, p. 33.

reasons why some might come and others might stay, many researchers, including Lee, believed that personality was a factor in migration. He said, "there are personalities which are resistant to change, change of residence as well as other changes, and there are personalities which welcome change for the sake of change" (1966, p. 51). Pierson agreed with Lee and added that the personalities that were attracted to migration were "saints and real sinners, fundamentalists and free thinkers" and believed that because of this America "never received its fair share of balanced, middle-of-the-road temperaments" (1973, p. 255).

The Golden Door

In addition to laws regulating who may leave or enter a country, migration is also controlled by *push* and *pull* factors (Litwak, 1960a; Sabagh, Van Arsdol, Jr., & Butler, 1969; Michelson, Belgue, & Stewart, 1973). These factors push one from one's own country and pull one to a country where the perceived opportunity lies. Some common push factors would be famine, over-population, oppression, wars, rebellions, and invasions. Pull factors are primarily a country willing to open its doors and in which one perceives that one's opportunity lies. According to Lee "it is not so much the actual factors at origin and destination as the perception of these factors which results in migration" (1966, p. 51). Millions of immigrants perceived the United States as the land of opportunity and, at the peak of immigration in 1907, over 1,200,000 immigrants entered what they hoped would be their golden door. "The golden door has appeared in one form or another in all cultures, in all times" (Sussman & Settles, 1993, p. 219), and represents what each individual hopes and longs for. Inscribed on the Statue of Liberty are the celebrated lines of Emma Lazarus:

> Give me your tired, your poor,
> your huddled masses, yearning to breathe free
> the wretched refuse of your teeming shore,
> send these, the homeless, tempest-tossed, to me
> I lift my lamp beside the golden door.

Some might have actually believed that the streets were paved with gold. Others who came believed simply that if people were willing to work long and hard, and they took advantage of every opportunity, then anything was possible. Upward mobility became equated with a willingness to move, with each move promising even more success (Shumaker & Stokols, 1982). This belief in the unlimited success available in the United States, along with the concept that each generation would continue to do better than the last was so common that it became known as the *American Dream* (Lang, 1988; Sussman, 1959).

The Family System During Assimilation

What happened to the immigrants and their families once through the golden door? Not all who came intended to stay. Some held the dream of returning home someday. For others, the first move was to be one of many. "A person who has once migrated; broken the bonds of family and left the place where one spent one's childhood is more likely to migrate again than the person who has never migrated" (Lee, 1966, p. 54).

The myth existed that America was a *melting pot*. That somehow "foreigners were swallowed up in bustling cities; they and their children were reconstituted into new Americans (while at the same time adding something of the Old World to American culture)" (Chudacoff, 1972, p. 63).

This myth has long been discarded and we know now that migration is not a solitary event but is a process over time (Brody, 1969; Sluzki, 1979). Some families assimilate quickly, and in the process find "it is necessary to discard former identifications (particularly those with parents and kin) for newer and more appropriate ones" (Sussman, 1959, p. 334).

Sussman also saw the "The breaking away of first generation members from their immigrant families as a necessary prelude to growth and assimilation into American society" (ibid.). During this assimilation process there are often greater than normal intergenerational differences as "children acquire the values, tastes and habits of the new culture faster than their parents" (Leslie, 1993, p. 199).

Leslie believes that there is often conflict between the generations and roles become blurred as children may act as translators which puts them in a power position and upsets the family dynamics. In addition, family members may enter the country at different times and their rates of acculturation may contribute to keeping the family off balance. When family members have left a young child behind with family members and the family is reunited years later, they may have difficulty in adjusting to the young adult who arrives.

"Some families manage to mourn what has been left behind and integrate it constructively into a blend of old and new rules, models, and habits that constitute their new reality" (Sluzki, 1979, p. 386). Sluzki believes that these families emerge from the migration process stronger than before. The families that idealize what they have left behind may become stuck in the mourning and loss stages and find themselves unable to adapt. Whatever has been avoided by the first generation must be dealt with by the second generation and this he says is "generally expressed as a clash between generations" (ibid., p. 389). By the third generation the family is often "indistinguishable from those of the area to which they have moved" (Glick, 1993 p. 42). The exceptions to this, according to Sluzki, would be those families sheltered or ghettoed by choice or force in their country of adoption.

The leaving behind of extended family members through the immigration/migration process may have actually prepared the family for the demands of the industrial system, a system that required the family to follow opportunity. In stripping the family of extended family members the family was better suited for the rapid mobility that was to follow (Lidz, 1963).

When American industry rapidly expanded following WWII and business had a need to move personnel, there was a population in place uniquely suited to fill that need. As descendants of largely lower middle class European immigrants unfamiliar with leisure, they had been instilled with a strong work ethic. Many had been away to war and, upon returning, left home again to acquire a college education on the GI bill. According to Marshall and Cooper "The first move away from home is the most difficult and those having moved once are more likely to move again" (1976 p. 203). Immigration may have played a part in the histories of these individuals' families making it more likely that they would view moving as opportunity, without realizing that moving can have negative effects as well.

CHAPTER IV

MOBILITY AND THE MYTH OF STABILITY

Mobility, change, and intergenerational differences have been more characteristic of families than exceptional in the history of the United States [1]

When corporate relocation began, it had been preceded by an era of stability following WWII that was not actually the norm for our society. According to Skolnick and Skolnick the postwar decade is considered by researchers who study that period as an "aberrant historical period" (in Walsh 1993, p. 13) and they believe it was the country's reaction to the Great Depression and WWII.

Researchers say that just as storytelling in ancient cultures transmitted folklore, today's parents along with researchers and public policy makers were socialized by television shows such as Father Knows Best, Leave it to Beaver and Ozzie and Harriet. All presented an idealized view of a stable and intact family life. At the time "three-fifths of American households conformed to the vision of modern nuclear family domesticity" (Walsh, 1993, p. 13). This image, of a house in the suburbs with dad as bread-winner and mom as homemaker, has persisted as the ideal American family, even though today this represents

[1] Hareven, in Settles (1993, p. 13). From an article based on an address given by Barbara H. Settles at the Groves Conference on Marriage and the Family in San Antonio, TX in April 1987.

"fewer than 8% of all households" (ibid., p. 16). We now know that many cultures have different family forms and that each culture believes their form to be ideal.

Before the decade of the fifties American families had been quite diverse, working as a broad collective unit and expanding as needed to include non-kin boarders, elderly relatives, and orphaned or delinquent children of relatives. The nostalgia for the past distorts reality, which was that the norm for the country has been one of constant movement and change.

The Superintendent of the Census predicted in 1850 that once the frontier was settled American mobility would decrease. However, by 1899 the migration data was consistent with earlier years and showed no signs of slowing down. As the country changed from frontier to agrarian, and then industrial, this movement continued. There were migrations from the farms to the cities and a significant one from the South to the North known as the *Great Migration*. From 1910 to 1930, over one million people of color made their way North in search of opportunity. This migration, while unnoticed by many, was one of the first indicators of the social changes that were to take place in the sixties. More recent general population movements have been to the Southwest and researchers predict that future movements will be to the West and South.

The continuing mobility was a concern to researchers. In 1936 Angell wrote, "The American family has been in a state of rapid transition, which has often been called disorganization, for at least fifty years" (p. 11). What was changing was not the numbers of Americans moving but how mobility was being regarded. Long and Boertlein observed that mobility, once seen as necessary for achieving success, was now looked upon as "an unfavorable trait in our national character" (in Shumaker & Stokols 1982, p. 3). In addition, it was the cause of the "disruption of family life and the disintegration of neighborhoods" (ibid., p. 2).

Throughout the twenties and thirties sociologists believed that "urban chaos was created by residential instability and by the heavy migration of rural, often foreign, immigrants to major cities" (Rossi & Shlay, 1982, p. 3). Mobility was focused on as the cause of the breakdown of community ties, which would result in an alienated society. The belief existed that rural communities had social controls and that a mobile population, now free of those controls, was the cause of social ills such as "juvenile delinquency, suicide, crime and prostitution" (ibid., p. 23). They further believed that if one could determine the cause of mobility, then all social ills would cease. As a result, the early research was focused on finding connections between mobility and social and psychiatric problems.

A 1937 study by Beach and Beach found transient populations less connected to their friends and communities, and studies by the University of Chicago found greater degrees of deviance and alienated behavior in transient populations. Researchers would later criticize the Chicago study for faulty methodology (Rossi & Shlay, 1982, p. 23). In contrast, another study in 1943 by Smith studied urban and rural mobile college students and found that the urban students were brighter due to heredity and environment. At the time socioeconomic factors were not accounted for. Later researchers were to find socioeconomic as well as educational levels significant in the study of the very complex factor of mobility. By the late 1940s there was sufficient conviction in government circles that research was needed and a federally funded study in the social psychology of urban residential mobility was undertaken.

This resulted in one of the first and most widely quoted works on residential mobility called Why Families Move (Rossi, 1955). Rossi explained that it pleased no one at the time because in doing the study he and his team used the now common, but at the time controversial, sample-survey method. This brought to light a different view of mobility than did earlier studies. The earlier studies, using clinical populations, observed greater deviance and alienation among transient populations. When Rossi's study, using general population samples, concluded that the moving was not due to normlessness but to changing family needs, and that there did not seem to be any adverse affects upon the family as a result of the moving, the results were unexpected (Rossi & Shlay, 1982). While these were within city and not the long distance moves associated with corporate relocation, later researchers such as DaVanzo (1977), Duncan and Newman, (1975), Lansing (1966), and Michelson (1977) supported Rossi's assertion that residential mobility at the time was a result of changing family needs and was not pathological in origin.

Several other researchers began studying the effects of mobility on school age children. Phillips, Shenker, and Revitz in 1951 studied how a new child assimilates into the group. They reported that the new child first observes the group, then slowly learns to mimic group behavior in an effort to be accepted by the group. This was a small study and not widely quoted. It is of interest because it describes the subtle processes of adaptation and behavior change. Mobile families use these patterns, learned in childhood and taken into adulthood, as they adapt hairstyles, clothing, speech, and behavior patterns in order to fit in with each new community.

In 1953 Downie reported comparable academic scores among movers and non-movers. He believed that earlier studies showing that mobile children did less well academically were better understood if one took into consideration the fact that different school districts had different procedures; records were frequently absent at time of transfer; and there was often school time lost during the move. Stubblefield (1955) reported on a number of children he was seeing in treatment for emotional problems; problems that he believed had been aggravated by a recent family move. The children had been given very little advance information regarding the move. The suddenness of the move and the fact that the children had not been allowed time or the opportunity to express their feelings about the move had brought on the symptoms of sleep disturbances, apathy, and behavior problems. He suggested that parents or caregivers should give the child a great deal of psychological support during the move, which would minimize the *traumatic effect* of the move on the child. A new idea in its day, it is widely accepted and commonly used today by those working in the relocation field.

Gordon and Gordon (1958) found rates of emotional disorders higher in mobile suburban areas. In addition, they concluded that boys suffered because the fathers' involvement at work meant less involvement at home. This in turn they said meant the wife was left trying to fill both roles and this caused strain and anxiety. While their study was not specifically focused on corporate families, something new was being observed by researchers that was relevant. Called at first "rural non-farm" or "fringe families" (Jaco & Belknap, 1953, p. 552), what was being observed and studied for the first time was suburban living.

In May 1953 William H. Whyte Jr. began a four part series for Fortune magazine called "The Transients." In this early look at what was to become a way of life for corporate families, Whyte detailed the lifestyle of the new breed of permanent transients. He observed that as they moved about, the more similar environments would become and therefore, the easier it would be to move repeatedly. What was also different about this mobility was that for the first time, it was a very visible and mainly middle class who was moving. Earlier movements had been largely immigrant and lower socioeconomic populations. The problem had always been that success did not automatically come as a result of moving. Moving was only one part of the equation:

> Horace Greeley, remember, gave two pieces of advice, not one: 'Go West, young man, and grow up with the country.' Thus it was onward and upward with the west! The West was a kind of elevator. One moved sideways in order to reach the elevator, then pressed the button for some higher floor. So in the end American mobility had to be vertical as well as lateral if it was to be judged a success. (Pierson, 1973, p. 12)

The corporate lifestyle, which merged geographic and social mobility, was the elevator that would take ambitious men and women upward to success in the second half of the twentieth century. How many stops there were depended on the corporation. One moved if one was loyal to the corporation, and loyalty to the corporation was the mantra of the fifties. Researchers may have had growing concerns about mobility, but their studies were largely unknown to the corporate families. What did reach the corporate population was Whyte's article and his quote by an executive, who said, "...we never make a man move. Of course, he kills his career if he doesn't. But we never make him do it" (1953a,

p. 117). The corporations had the answer to how success was to be achieved. The questions would not come until the next decade.

CHAPTER V

THE 60s: DECADE OF TURBULENCE

The basic conflict is not between the individual (or family) and society, but between the classes who live together in a bureaucratized political and cultural democracy. The prime challenge is how to live with bureaucracy; how to use it rather than be used by it; how to obtain individual freedom and social resources from it through political action [1]

America in the 60s

The sixties was a decade of enormous political and social change. Television, that had once brought stories of the idealized families of the fifties, now brought images of political assassinations, war, protest, and civil rights marches. People of color questioned why they were being excluded from America's promise of opportunity. Their time had come and the country would listen. Women also questioned their roles and place in society but change would come slowly and equal rights for women would still be debated decades later. The generation that was expected to go to war questioned the country's right to send them. "Hell no, we won't go"! was a familiar chant as they protested in the streets that they wanted peace, not war. Confrontations with authorities were frequent and sometimes violent.

[1] H. J. Gans in his 1967 book The Levittowners, p. 418.

Hippie, *flower child*, *LSD*, and *commune* became part of the vocabulary and the peace movement grew. Many turned to consciousness raising sessions in a search for self-fulfillment. The generation gap was evident as the organization man and his children in love beads tried to communicate. Puritan values and free love clashed the country over.

Once again, the family was changing. Unmarried couples, both gay and straight, lived together openly. Others formed loose extended family type living arrangements called communes where they supported themselves by selling their crafts and artwork. This group shunned the corporate life and its materialistic goals. Their goals were peace and love. Equally clear on their goals, those who chose the corporate world were career driven and success oriented. Success for them was defined as getting to the top of their profession and enjoying the financial rewards it would bring. The two lifestyles appeared to be at opposite ends of the spectrum. However, by the end of the decade many changes would have taken place. Some progress would be made in both civil and women's rights. America's space program would be successful and man would walk on the moon. The country would still be at war, but some would leave the communes and enter the business world. They might now be dressed for success but they would bring their values with them. By the end of the next decade they would be among the first to question the corporations, just as they had questioned the government. Other changes would take place as well; one in the composition of the work force, as women and minorities slowly entered professional careers; the other in the economy, which after years of prosperity began to decline. All three would forever change the way the family and corporations viewed relocation.

Stress Studies in the 60s

Mobility is still the focus of many studies but *stress* enters as a factor aided by a research tool developed at this time. "The early work of Holmes and Rahe (1967), more than anything else, provided investigators with a basic approach to measurement whereby the large proximal social field could be assessed for relatively discrete and contemporaneous occurrences capable of engendering personal stress" (Liem & Liem, in Dohrenwend & Dohrenwend, 1984, p. 234).

The "Social Readjustment Rating Scale" (Table 1) commonly called the *Holmes and Rahe Stress Test*, measured levels of a stress reaction to life events. Holmes and Rahe examined over 5000 U.S. Navy medical records looking for events associated with either an injury or the onset of an illness. A list of 43 events was compiled. They were then mailed to a sample of 394 professionals who ranked them, and the final list was compiled. Point values were assigned to each life event. The life events ranged from number 1, "Death of spouse," assigned the highest stress points (100), to number 43, "Minor violations of the law," assigned only 11

Table 1. Social Readjustment Rating Scale

(Holmes & Rahe, 1967, p. 216)

Rank	Life event	Mean value
1	Death of spouse	100
2	Divorce	73
3	Marital separation	65
4	Jail term	63
5	Death of close family member	63
6	Personal injury or illness	53
7	Marriage	50
8	Fired at work	47
9	Marital reconciliation	45
10	Retirement	45
11	Change in health of family member	44
12	Pregnancy	40
13	Sex-difficulties	39
14	Gain of new family member	39
15	Business readjustment	39
16	Change in financial state	38
17	Death of close friend	37
18	Change to different line of work	36
19	Change in number of arguments with spouse	35
20	Mortgage over $10,000	31
21	Foreclosure of mortgage or loan	30
22	Change in responsibilities at work	29
23	Son or daughter leaving home	29
24	Trouble with in-laws	29
25	Outstanding personal achievement	28
26	Wife begin or stop work	26
27	Begin or end school	26
28	Change in living conditions	25
29	Revision of personal habits	24
30	Trouble with boss	23
31	Change in work hours or conditions	20
32	Change in residence	20
33	Change in schools	20
34	Change in recreation	19
35	Change in church activities	19
36	Change in social activities	18
37	Mortgage or loan less than $10,000	17
39	Change in sleeping habits	16
39	Change in number of family get-togethers	15
40	Change in eating habits	15
41	Vacation	13
42	Christmas	12
43	Minor violations of the law	11

stress points. "Scoring over 300 points in one year had an 80% risk of becoming seriously ill or depressed. Scores between 200 and 300 carried a 50% risk. People accumulating 150 points during the previous six months felt stressed" (Meltzer & Grandjean, 1989, p. 8).

A "Change of residence" only rated 20 points. However, when all the changes involved in a relocation were totaled, the cumulative stress points would be in the crisis range.

Holmes and Rahe believed that what produced the illness was the amount of change required. Too much change would overload one's ability to cope, and illness would follow. Rahe said later that it was not really a new concept and that the "observation that an individual's health may suffer following a wide variety of recent life stresses is nearly as old as the history of medicine itself" and dated back to Greek and Babylonian times (Rahe, in Dohrenwend & Dohrenwend, 1984[2] , p. 48).

It is a useful tool in working with relocating families not only to demonstrate the pile-up of stressors that may occur in a relocation, but also that *good* things, such as "an outstanding personal achievement" or a promotion that brings a "change in responsibility at work" may bring on stress. It is also important to remember that it is not the Life Events in themselves that are stressful, but one's perception of an event as stressful or not. From a systems perspective, if one member perceives the life event to be stressful, the interaction will affect the entire family system.

[2] A decade earlier Alvin Toffler explored this same theme in his novel, Future Shock.

Several studies mention stress in the sixties. For example, Jennings discusses the stress of frequent relocations as managers are moved as often as "four times in six years" (1967, p. 72). He concludes, that while it was a cause of strain on the family system, it was not specifically a cause of divorce.

In a study by Lehr and Hendrickson (1968) on how adolescents deal with relocation stress, they reported that the boys appeared to miss their friends more and the girls appeared more adept at making new friends. In addition, the children perceived their fathers as happier about the move than their mothers. Researchers would later repeat these observations.

Levine would also mention stress. He quotes a study by Kantor saying, "evidence would support a view of a move as a stressful situation with some likelihood of being associated with mental disturbance in adults in the United States" (Kantor, in Levine, 1966, p. 65). Three years earlier, in 1963, Kantor had written Mobility and Mental Health, following the fifth annual conference on Community Mental Health. In it she says previous associations between mental illness and migration may have been a product of the cultural setting in which the migration was taking place. For example, immigrants frequently were scattered throughout the country with no support groups. Unfamiliar with the language and customs they often suffered from culture shock. Many were from cultures that encouraged group dependency. American culture encourages independence and autonomy. Thus, Americans frequently misinterpreted this type of group dependency.

Levine said Kantor also reported that "teachers rate mobile children as less well adjusted than non-mobile children" (ibid.) and that she suggests families with problem children may move in order to find another school or neighborhood to alleviate the problem. Levine failed to mention that Kantor had added there might be other problems such as marital discord that might affect the child's adjustment. In addition, Kantor added that her findings only concerned mobility within a metropolitan area and could not be generalized to long-distance mobility (Kantor, 1963). The majority of corporate relocations are in the category of long-distance moves.

Mobility Studies in the 60s

In 1960 Litwak published two companion papers in which he was looking at social mobility, or moving through social classes, and geographic mobility, moving through distance. It is commonly believed that a geographic move harms family ties. Litwak refuted this and found that the distance the family lived from one another, or a change in social class, did not prevent the family from staying in contact. Even though family members did not see each other as frequently they had in the past, they could, and frequently did, retain close family ties. He believed the studies that found otherwise had been done on small town, ethnic, or working class groups. Litwak believed in the "modified extended" family which he defined as "a series of nuclear families bound together on an egalitarian basis, with a strong emphasis on these extended family bonds as an end value" (Litwak, 1960a, p. 10). He suggested that this form was stronger than the isolated nuclear family, more egalitarian than the classic extended family, and was the desired family form of the future.

In another look at family moves, Switzer, Hirschberg, Myers, Gray, Evers and Forman (1961) found that following a move "each child suffers, at least temporarily, an impairment of capacity to cope with his life situation and to make interpersonal contact" (p. 529). They also reported a systems effect, which is that the parents, not feeling comfortable in the new location, spoke negatively of the area and did not interact in the community. As the parents became more depressed, they became withdrawn and emotionally less available to the child. The child's reaction to the community then became a negative one as well. Switzer et al. believed that what the child suffered from was the loss of the parents during the move, not the move itself. Once the dynamics were understood, the researchers concluded that if immediate preventative interventions took place serious problems could be avoided.

A behavior change in adolescents affecting their ability to make close friends and depression following a relocation would be recurring themes in the decades ahead.

Other researchers reporting on social and geographic mobility were Morris, Pestaner, and Nelson. In a 1967 study they reported that when a family moves up the social ladder or to an unfamiliar place the parents isolation and insecurity will be communicated to the child. In addition, some teachers in their study stated that academic performance was also affected. Morris et al. reported that Gilliland, in a review of 17 studies on the relationship of mobility and achievement, found that the conflicting results were because I.Q. and socioeconomic status were not taken into account systematically. They called for a study of the "relationship of mobility to individual achievement, taking the achievement motivation and value system of the family into account" (Morris, et al., 1967, p. 79). In addition, they suggested that a curriculum be developed to fulfill the needs of the mobile child. The family as a more tightly closed system, and the socioeconomic and I.Q. levels as variables in mobility, would become the focus of future studies.

Weiss believed that the "primary problem of geographic mobility is the sense of social isolation inevitably created by the loss of established relationships and the deficit of new relationships" (1969, p. 66). Brody (1969) agreed, and said that a move also involves new places and new norms to adjust to. Brody added that there are also those who move as a way of dealing with personal problems and they would find that their problems moved with them. Social isolation and the loss of established relationships will be two of the most often cited problems associated with relocation.

Mobility and Place

In Fried's study of the West Enders of Boston, a group of working class families was relocated when their homes were condemned by the city. Their attachment to their old neighborhood elicited a strong and unexpected grief reaction as long as two years after the move. Fried concluded from his study that one has a sense of spatial identity; that *place* forms a part of one's identity. The place he was referring to was not the larger city of Boston but a very specific area and locale within the city. It was only this place that felt like home to this group of people. Fried believed that being relocated fragmented the interpersonal relationships and group networks that were formed in that place. The grief and sense of loss was not for the relationships but for the actual physical location, the place itself (in Duhl, 1963). *Grief* and *a sense of loss* will also be frequently repeated themes in future decades.

In another study of place and its involvement in the relocation process, Gans (in Duhl, 1963) looked at the effect that the move from the city to the suburbs had on families. He said that critics of the suburbs argued that the suburbs made people too conforming and that there was too much socializing. Gans believed that the suburbs did not bring about the changes, but were the reasons for moving there in the first place. He agreed with Brody that people took their problems with them wherever they moved.

Gans later did a study of one of the first suburbs called Levittown, in New Jersey. He said that Whyte's[3] articles in the fifties had created a "myth of suburbia" which was "keeping down with the Joneses" (1967, p. xv). Newcomers, he said, were encouraged not to keep their lawn too well tended or dress up too much. Other articles added to the myth until the consensus was that the suburbs mass-produced people like the houses they lived in. In order to study and understand how a suburban culture grows and develops Gans moved into Levittown[4] himself and was one of the first occupants. He found that,

> what brought a community into being in Levittown was not the preoccupancy aspirations of the residents, but rather a complex process of external initiative and subsequent internal transformation that produced organizations and institutions which reflected the backgrounds of the majority of the population. (1967, p. 141)

Gans also defended the suburbs and said that what outsiders perceived as blandness and dullness made it a comfortable place to live. He believed that what made a place like Greenwich Village exciting to outsiders might be

[3] William H. Whyte, Jr. writing the series 'The Transients' in Fortune magazine between May and August of 1953.

[4] Before WWII two-thirds of U.S. citizens were renters. After WWII two-thirds became home owners. Levittown and a number of other suburbs grew after WWII largely due to the GI Bill. As part of legislation passed in 1944 the returning service personnel were guaranteed loans that enabled them to purchase homes. William Levitt's marketing was targeted directly to this group (Odyssey film archives, The GI Bill, Karen Thomas producer, PBS 1997).

the very things that would make it uncomfortable to live in, such as the noise and traffic.

Studies Showing Positive Results

Some studies claimed that moving had positive effects. Greene and Daughty (1961) reported in their study of mobile high school juniors that they had higher than average grade placement scores on the California Arithmetic Achievement Test and fewer days absent from school. Therefore, the researchers reported mobility as having a favorable effect on their subjects. Evans reported in 1966 that the mobile children had "better records in reading and science, although the superiority was small" (p. 22). Landis and Stoetger, also in 1966, found no apparent problems among relocating families. And in Cedar Rapids, Iowa, Burchinal found "few if any serious adverse effects" (1963, p. 11) resulting from the family move. Burchinal compared three groups of children in grades seven and eleven. Children moving in from farms and children moving in from other cities were compared to a third local group who had never moved. In finding no significant differences he further interpreted that "persons who learn to cope with family moves when they are children may be better prepared to face the complexities of family moves as adults" (ibid., p. 12). A number of other researchers will also mention the positive results of mobility.

Discussion

Just as the early studies appeared to be looking for connections between mental illness and mobility, the studies in the sixties showed trends as well.

Depression, isolation, stress, grief, and a sense of loss are all mentioned as relating to mobility in this decade. Researchers are also beginning to observe behavior changes in adolescents and changes in the family system due to moving. All of these will be trends in the decades ahead.

The conflicting results of some studies indicate that mobility may not be as simple a factor to study as first believed. The importance of considering socioeconomic level, education level, and I.Q. in future studies is mentioned and will be used when the focus is on corporate relocation. Later researchers will in fact find that there are many variables that affect mobility and, if not accounted for, will confound results.

Another trend is that mobility statistics show a slight decline in the sixties. The annual mobility rate dropped from 19.9% to 18.7%. While still a relatively high rate, researchers began to speculate if the rates were due to social changes, were unrelated, or were the beginning of a downward trend (Shumaker & Stokols, 1982). It will prove to be a slight downward trend for the nation but corporate moves are on the rise. In the mid-1960s, it was estimated that 296,000 employees were relocated, and by the mid-1970s that number rose to 750,000 (Sell, 1982).

From the moving statistics it is clear that there were corporate families moving, but no clear distinction is made in these early studies of which include corporate families and which do not. As such, it is not possible to draw valid conclusions regarding the effect of mobility on corporate families.

As corporate moving statistics show a dramatic increase in the next decade, corporate families become the focus of studies and a great deal is learned about the process of relocation and its impact on the family. It will raise many troubling questions for corporate families and their mobile lifestyle.

CHAPTER VI

THE 70s: THE ME GENERATION

The present breed of top managers is the first generation of mobile managers. They believe, strongly, in the 'efficacy of mobility.' In effect the social, psychological and economic values placed on success have spawned a generation of managers whose central concern is for mobility. To them, mobility is not only a means to an end, it has become an end in itself[1]

The label that the writer Tom Wolfe and others put on the young adults of the seventies was *The Me Generation.* On the surface it appears to mean selfishness as opposed to altruism, but in reality it "highlights the prevalence of the private struggles being enacted within our culture" (McCollum, 1990, p. 30). The label and the struggle were acknowledging the change taking place within society, a shift in values from outside loyalties to loyalty to oneself.

The family form was changing as well. Single mothers and fathers were choosing to raise children alone, and divorce and remarriages were blending families who struggled to reorganize into one family system. Two sets of rules, roles, and routines were expected to merge magically into one. Families would find the task more difficult than

[1] Louis V. Imundo, Jr. in his 1974 article for Personnel Journal, 'Problems associated with managerial mobility,' p. 910.

first envisioned but, as their numbers increased, society would grow more supportive of their struggle.

For society in general if one word could be used to sum up the decade it might be *disillusionment*. There was disillusionment on the part of the American public who lost confidence in elected officials as political scandals rocked the nation. One called *Watergate* destroyed many political careers and the suffix *gate* would be attached to scandals for decades to come.

The Vietnam veterans were disillusioned. The war had ended, but unlike the fifties, those who had fought returned to no heroes' welcome and no waiting jobs. Instead, the country appeared to want to forget the war and the veterans as quickly as possible. Many became bitter and *Post Traumatic Stress Disorder* was the name that identified their struggle.

There was disillusionment on the part of women and minorities when their career and salary progress was slower than they had expected. Laws had been enacted but years of discrimination would not be erased overnight. Words like *token*, *quotas*, and *glass ceiling* were heard and seen in print, and the success of the few gave hope to many that change would eventually occur.

Mobile corporate families were disillusioned as a recession brought inflation and a poor housing market that eroded any financial profits, one of the main incentives of moving. In addition, wives of mobile executives were finding that frequent moving enhanced their husband's career but hindered their own. Dual-career became the term of choice for two professional families who now had two careers to consider when moving instead of one.

The executive level of corporate America was now filled with loyal employees who had benefited from their willingness to move. This reinforced their belief in the efficacy of moving; that moving broadened and seasoned employees for greater responsibilities and was good for their careers. But, the employees they were attempting to transfer were the children of the 60s and 70s whose driving force was now self-fulfillment, not getting to the top. *Quality of life* was about battle it out with *loyalty to the corporation*.

Focusing the Spotlight on Corporate Relocation

The decade opened with three authors contributing to the belief that moving was a traumatic experience. Social critic Alvin Toffler wrote in Future Shock that corporate relocation was the largest migration in our nations history; a migration that began after WWII and continued still. He believed that America had become a nation of nomads and that, unless man learned to control the rate of change, society was "doomed to a massive adaptational breakdown" (1971, p. 2).

The following year Vance Packard published A Nation of Strangers whose theme was rootlessness. Packard wrote of his belief that man needed a sense of community for shaping his own identity, self-esteem, and well-being. He stated that "at least 40 million Americans now lead feebly rooted lives" (1972, p. 2) and that this rootlessness was a cause for alarm bringing with it isolation, social fragmentation, and a "society coming apart at the seams" (ibid.).

This was immediately followed in 1973 by psychiatrist Robert Seidenberg's book Corporate Wives/ Corporate Casualties. He wrote that the repeated uprooting of the corporate life shattered the identities and sense of self-worth of corporate wives. Seidenberg believed that his clients felt isolated, grieved for what they had lost, and were depressed, all as a result of their mobile lifestyle.

The three books made the best seller lists and Toffler's book alone sold over five million copies the first year. They had their critics who said that they "generalized grossly from the studies they cited, and their books, newspaper and magazine articles were written to sell the idea that mobility is damaging to the well-being of the American family" (Brett, 1982, p. 450). Gans also said of Packard's book that he "implied they were typical even though they sound quite atypical" (1967, p. 25) and that he presented an "exaggerated picture of mobility and its negative effects" (ibid., p. 26).

These three books served to put the spotlight directly on corporate mobility. They were frequently quoted and, as a result, many studies followed which explored the problems highlighted by these authors.

Seidenberg, the most quoted of the three, was cited in: Ammons, Nelson, and Wodarski (1982), Bayes (1989), Berry (1985), Brett (1982), Carter (1981), Friedman (1989), Gaylord and Symons (1986), Gullotta and Donohue (1981b), Keith and Schafer (1980), Levenson and Hollmann (1980), Levin, Groves, and Lurie (1980), Loomis (1992), McCollum (1990), Nida and Heller (1987), Olson and Brown (1986), Puskar (1986), Renshaw (1976), Schetky (1982), Starker (1988), Stokols and Shumaker (1982), and Voydanoff (1980).

Packard in: Ammons, Nelson, and Wodarski (1982), Asher (1980), Brett (1982), Friedman (1989), Hendershott (1995), Hyman (1984), Jalongo (1985), Kroger (1980), McCollum (1990), Pinder (1989), and Starker (1988).

Toffler in: Brett (1982), Carter (1981), Donohue (1983), Friedman (1989), Hendershott (1995), and Hyman (1984).

The number of authors who quoted Seidenberg, Packard, and Toffler serve to illustrate how widely read these authors were. Their beliefs may have influenced society's perception of relocation at the beginning of the decade. Once again, unaware that mobility had been written about for decades, writers and researchers appeared to be focused on providing solutions to this new problem of American mobility. This time, however, the focus was not on the broader concept of mobility but specifically corporate mobility.

The Beginning of the Corporate Relocation Studies

The theme of *depression and loss* which was touched

upon in the 60s and highlighted by Seidenberg, was now picked up by several researchers and directly linked to moving. The premise of Seidenberg's book was that the husband's credentials were transferable but the wife had to start over from the bottom again and again. He believed that wives of successful men often became defeated and were seen "clinically during their third and fourth decades of life chronically depressed, lacking in hope or desire and frequently addicted to alcohol, tranquilizers, and barbiturates" (1973, p. 2).

The study that Seidenberg quoted, in addition to his own clients' case histories, was a 1972 study by Weissman and Paykel on "Moving and depression in women." This Yale study was also quoted by Vandervelde (1979) in her book on corporate wives, and by Weiss (1973) in his book on social isolation. What these writers said they had found interesting about the study was the researchers' observations on mobility.

Weissman and Paykel had concluded that moving was such a part of American society, and so taken for granted, that the women never associated their symptoms of depression with recent moves. The researchers further stated that they believed that it was the multiple losses of social networks, familiar living patterns, security, and work that contributed to the depression. Social pressure inhibited the acceptance of stress and the women "internalized the stresses and blamed themselves for their problems. The result was the emergence of depressive symptoms" (1972, p. 24).

Weissman and Paykel reached several conclusions. First, they said, "in some cases the move was the last straw in a series of stressful events and interpersonal difficulties" (ibid.) indicating that there might be a pile-up of stressors and not simply one move or one stressful event.

Second, that the pattern of depression was evident even when the moves were voluntary and due to what would normally be considered desirable circumstances, such as a new house or promotion. They said that this contradicted earlier reports, "suggesting that moves produce detrimental effects only if they are involuntary or undesirable" (ibid.).

Third, that the impact of moving was stressful to women of all socioeconomic groups, not just the working class as previous studies indicated. This may have been a reference to Fried's 1962 study on families in the West End of Boston. Fried had found grief symptoms following ~~relocation but~~ said at the time that it applied only to this working class group and could not be generalized to any other population. Now, studies were finding negative effects of mobility in the middle class corporate populations as well.

Several of the conclusions reached by Weissman and Paykel may be particularly relevant to corporate mobility. The first, is that moving is so taken for granted as a life-style in the corporate world that symptoms related to a move would be easily overlooked. The second, ~~is~~ that corporate moves are frequently promotions, made under what would be considered desirable circumstances, and therefore perceived as good for the family. If people are not aware that *good* things can also be stressful, they blame themselves for not coping well with the move. The third, that families today cope with many issues when moving that were relatively unknown to the nuclear families of the fifties. For example, divorce and remarriage may mean complicated custody arrangements. There may be dual-career, eldercare, and daycare issues, all of which can lead to a pile up of stress that the relocating family may be unprepared for.

Even when a pile-up of stress occurs, corporate families are reluctant to seek outside help and frequently put the needs of the corporation ahead of their own. This observation was made by Marshall and Cooper (1976) and Pahl and Pahl (1971). This reluctance to discuss their personal problems with outsiders, as well as their pattern of putting the needs of the corporation ahead of their own, may put corporate families at risk during a move.

Grief and the Stages of Relocation in the 70s

Kübler-Ross's stages of grief and loss are referred to in this decade as relating to relocation. Constable says, "a move is something like a death. A part of us dies, is separated, and we mourn" (1978, p. 419). Constable goes on to say that we grieve and experience a bittersweet sense of loss as we search for what it is we feel that we have lost.

A similar view was expressed by Werkman who said that mobility brings with it, "a definite experience of mourning" (1979, p. 176) as well as the necessity of recognizing that it is impossible to return to the life known before.

Friedrich and Hultstrand (1978) and Gaylord (1979) also referred to a period of grief following a move. Gaylord added that because a *good* corporate wife does not feel or express anger at being uprooted, she is at risk for developing depression by suppressing these emotions. Gaylord was one of several researchers who cited Weissman and Paykel's 1972 study on relocation and depression in women.

Viney and Bazeley (1977) did a related study on Australian women and relocation. They concluded that the loss of physical objects resulted in outward directed aggression, but the loss of personal and social objects brought feelings of loneliness and inadequacy. While the study was not on American women it was particularly interesting because it may be that what is actually lost may be relevant to how the loss is perceived, and therefore affects how one reacts to the loss.

Marshall and Cooper in a British study of mobile families believed that the separation of family members during the relocation was stressful, and said husbands in their study believed that "the wife bears the brunt of moving" (1976, p. 196). Factors that they believed important in the family's adjustment were; the family's initial attitude toward the move, the family's life cycle stage, and personality type. Those who looked forward to the move, and had less emotional ties to an area and fewer family commitments, found moving to new places exciting. On the whole, this group experienced satisfactory moves. Those who said that they did not like upheaval and instability in their lives, were not ready to move again, or had concerns about the effects of moving on their children, experienced less satisfactory moves. "Common to all types of wives were feelings of loneliness during the first few months in a new location" (ibid., p. 204).

Loneliness, Isolation, and Anomie in the 70s

Loneliness, isolation, and anomie as a result of mobility are frequent themes in the 70s. The terms *eunomia* and *anomia* are derived from the Greek. Eunomia means a well ordered condition in a society or state, the latter its opposite (Srole, 1956a). They are most often described as a continuum, with connectedness at one end and alienation on the other: A self-to-others scale.

Bean, Bonjean, and Burton state "The notion that social mobility disrupts and weakens social integration has a rich history in sociology" (1974, p. 62). Bean said that as the mobile individual cuts off the ties that bind him to his place he becomes less attached to anything and anybody. When Seidenberg used Durkheim's term *anomie* to describe the alienation that can occur in mobile populations the term was not new, but the application to corporate populations was (1973, p. 28).

Following Seidenberg's lead, loneliness, isolation, and anomie become frequent themes in the seventies. Vandervelde in her 1979 book on corporate wives said that it was not hard to see how anomie developed when the wife felt rootless and alienated after many moves. The wife feels there is no point to making friends and getting involved as she will get hurt when she has to leave again. Vandervelde described it as "committing emotional suicide" (p. 199).

Many researchers focused on women for alienation testing because society socializes women to be the nurturer and to take over the responsibility for the emotional well-being of the family. McKain reported that women who were functioning well reported "a surge of social activity following a move" and "alienated women seem not to reach out for inclusion as readily" (1973, p. 209). McKain's study was on a group of military wives in clinical treatment.

Weiss referred to these same feelings of social isolation stating, that when those in transition do not share their new situation with family and friends they "may develop a sense of marginality to their community" (in Caplan & Killilea, 1976, p. 216).

In an earlier work, Weiss (1973) described social isolation as a lack of a network of kinfolk, neighbors, or friends. This differs from the emotional isolation that one may experience with the loss of an intimate tie of a spouse, lover, parent, or child. The experience of emotional isolation is believed solved only with the finding of a replacement for the significant relationship lost. The feeling of social isolation is believed to be more easily solved when, in time, one makes new friends and establishes ties in a community.

Researchers who work with alienated groups within society note that total alienation more frequently occurs in the downwardly mobile who cannot accept their situation. Anomie and alienation are also terms used in clinical populations to describe individuals with severe mental conditions such as schizophrenia, literally meaning the breakdown of an individuals sense of attachment to society. Some believe that it is more accurately used to describe a "state of mind" not a "state of society" (McKain, 1973, p. 206). However, mobility was believed to erode the ties of community and kinship which protected one from the pervasive feelings of isolation and anomie (Gordon, 1976).

A Sense of Community – Gemeinschaft and Gesellschaft

When Packard wrote that an "individual needs a sense of community. . . for shaping his own sense of identity. . . self-esteem and well-being" (1972, p. x), he was alluding to the age old concepts of *Gemeinschaft* and *Gesellschaft*.

Gemeinschaft could be described as the community which functions as a unit based on the ties of kin and those kindred of spirit. Gesellschaft is the larger society as a whole where one might trade by agreement for goods and services.

Gemeinschaft was thought of as a living organism, while Gesellschaft was thought of as mechanical and artificial. From Confucius to Plato and Aristotle "in varied forms the categories continued to function in the writings of the social thinkers of the later centuries" (Sorokin, in Tönnies, 1957, p. ix). Tönnies, beginning in 1887, wrote extensively on the subject and believed that man "would unfold his essence only by living in communities of kinship, space (neighborhood), and spirit" (ibid., p. xi), but that he was also capable of functioning in the wider sphere to meet his remaining needs.

Sorokin wrote, that at the present time most intelligent men understand the "hidden weaknesses of the Gesellschaft type of society and man have grown to such an extent that the type is in deepest crisis and is crumbling before our very eyes" (ibid., p. x). It is interesting to note that the year was 1957 when Sorokin wrote this, a time often cited for its stability not its crumbling.

Packard was not the only writer in the 70s to write of the need for community. Toney in a 1976 study on mobility said that it took eleven years to establish roots in a community[2]. Other researchers believed that it took between one and two years to feel at home in a community. What writers appeared to be saying was that they found this new mobility to be threatening. If Americans were moving so fast that they could not establish roots then the very concept of community could become meaningless and the sense of

[2] Toney was quoting a 1974 study by Newman.

community believed necessary to nourish man might disappear.

Stress and the Family System in the 70s

The research on life events and illness that began in the 60s showed that stress negatively affected one's health and well-being. Studies had indicated that coronary heart disease was four times higher in mobile white collar males 35 to 45 years of age than blue collar stable males (Syme, Borhani & Buechley, 1965; Syme, Hyman & Enterline, 1965).

The '70s' studies continued to show that men who experience life events characterized by change are more susceptible to coronary heart disease than men who experience fewer such events (Holmes & Masuda, 1974, in Dohrenwend & Dohrenwend, 1984; House, 1974; Rabkin & Streuning, 1976). However, Glass in 1977 demonstrated that a Type A behavior is a behavior pattern associated with competitiveness, a sense of time urgency, and hostility. Glass found that it is the interaction of these behaviors that brings about the heart attack not simply change itself. Other researchers connected this pattern of behavior with heart attacks as well (Jenkins, Zyzanski, & Rosenman, 1976; Rosenman, Brand, Jenkins, Friedman, Straus, & Wurm, 1975). Imundo (1974) said, that contrary to popular belief, men who are *passed over* for promotions or transfers, actually experience more stress reactions, heart attacks, and suicides than those who receive the promotions.

Imundo also discussed the family system during relocation. He said that the husband and wife often feel differently about the move, which can cause marital conflict. The promotion may mean a change in status for one and not the other, which can create tension. The move will most often be made for one partners upwardly mobile career. The relocating employee also feels stress, as they must prove themselves in each new location. In addition, the children "easily sense their parents' tensions and anxieties, and in turn develop their own" (1974, p. 913).

Picking up on the stress theme from a systems perspective Piotrkowski examined the effect of what she called carryover stress from the work system to the family system. She referred to the worker as occupying a boundary role between the two systems and believed that there were "elaborate interchanges" (1979, p. 14) taking place affecting both systems. Piotrkowski found three patterns of carry-over. One, a positive carryover when enjoyment of work resulted in positive energy being brought home. Two, a negative carryover, when negative energy was brought home which would result in a stressful home environment. Three, an energy deficit, when the worker was so energy depleted by work that they are emotionally unavailable to the family. The reverse pattern of carryover from home to work also applied.

The Myth of Separate Worlds

Piotrkowski also mentioned Kanter and her "myth of separate worlds" (ibid., p. 206). This was the belief that work and the family occupied two separate and distinct planes with neither affecting the other. Piotrkowski agreed with Kanter that there was interchange between the two and said "even when people think that they are leaving work-related concerns at the job by not talking about them at home, such worries may be communicated unconsciously" (ibid.).

Kanter (1977) in her interviews of corporate families found the husband's role in the family was not clearly defined. She believed that the husband was subjected to stress in entering and exiting from the family system and that relocation intensified this stress. Boss (1977) agreed, although her studies focused on military families. She believed that a family needed to feel secure about who was inside the family system and who was outside, both physically and psychologically, for the family to function well. Military families frequently have longer separations and corporate families shorter, but more frequent ones.

Aldous, Osmond, and Hicks (1979) in studying work and family stress said that there was less marital satisfaction when the husband was either very successful or unsuccessful. When the husband was very successful, he used the power derived from his position to avoid family responsibility because often he found his work more fulfilling. Unsuccessful men felt the loss of power at work and this reduced their ability to function at home. Both situations caused stress in the family system. Believing that the two worlds are separate obscures the connections between the two. The result is that people blame themselves if the family is stressed and unhappy without realizing the systems interaction taking place.

In another study that mentioned stress and family systems, Boss, McCubbin, and Lester observed that the husbands "exits and returns require constant change in family system boundaries and role assignments" (1979, p. 80). They believed that this required frequent reorganization of the family system and was potentially highly stressful. In their study they found that some women "cope so well that they deny being stressed at all" (ibid.). In explaining this finding, they cited a stress model by Burr on family vulnerability that took into account the family's perception of change. "If the corporate wife buys into the corporate life-style and likes it, vulnerability to stress is decreased, since she views the situation as enjoyable rather than stressful" (ibid., p. 84). Again, one's perception of an event as a stressor or not affects the family's reaction to the event as stressful or not.

Perception and the subjective meaning that an event holds for an individual was mentioned by Renshaw:

> The research data indicate that the amount of influence an individual perceives that he has over events in a stressful situation is central to explaining why one individual is able to cope

> successfully with stressful events and another has difficulty with similar events. It also explains why a person is able to cope one time and has difficulty with a similar stressful situation at another time. (1976, p. 159)

Renshaw believed that the myth of separate work and family systems contributed to the cultural orientation of trying to establish cause for events. "Organizational events are blamed for family problems, and family events are blamed for organizational problems" (ibid., p. 154). Renshaw believed that the effects were systemic with the interaction affecting both systems. Also, that because individual perception was so subjective that "no two individuals or no two families would react exactly the same way to similar sets of potentially stressful events in organizational or family life" (ibid., p. 158).

Family Coping Behaviors

Mobility Syndrome is the term used by Imundo (1974) to describe changes in the behavior patterns and roles of mobile families. Imundo said that after a few relocations families become uncomfortable with long-term intimate relationships outside the family. They develop transient superficial relationships with outsiders. This comes about because it is painful to keep leaving friends behind. In order to avoid the pain a pattern develops of keeping people at a distance, which leads to more superficial relationships. These relationships may not be as satisfying and meaningful as deeper more intimate friendships. One may have many such casual friends and yet not understand why these friendships are not satisfying.

McCubbin, Dahl, Lester, and Ross (1975) studied coping behaviors and concluded that, as strategies for dealing with stress, some coping behaviors worked better that others. At times of stress, all families revert to their own coping behaviors. They believed that those families who closed ranks did better during stressful times than those who did not. This may serve the family well during the actual move. The problem is that the pattern may become the only one the family functions with and they may be too closed to outside relationships. Frequently, families develop patterns of behavior within their families of origin and may not be aware that these learned behaviors can and need to be changed. Frequently, the employee becomes preoccupied with work following a move and the relocating partner cuts themself off from their family and previous support systems. McCubbin et al. believes that this creates stress and conflict within the family system at a time when the family does not have the adaptive resources to withstand it.

Burr (1973) said that those families that viewed an adjustment as a challenge and were assertive in their approach adjusted more rapidly. This is only one example of a coping pattern that can be taught to mobile families. As for friendship, loneliness is like hunger. Instead of food, it is a signal to the psyche that emotional needs are not being met. The feeling may cause distress, but once it is understood the pattern can be broken. Families can be taught new coping styles and patterns of behavior that will better equip them to not only cope with the stress of a relocation but have more satisfying relationships as well.

Stress studies in this decade begin to show that men and women handle and process stress differently. Studies appear to place men at greater risk for heart attacks and women for depression. In addition, studies on family coping patterns indicate that some habits and patterns may be unhealthy for the relocating family and dropping them may lead to improved functioning.

Changing Values

Negative reports of mobility may have influenced the transferees and caused some to rethink relocation, but there were other factors at work as well. One was the economy. A recession brought not only a slowdown in home sales but also reduced housing prices resulting in financial losses for transferees. In an attempt to save money the corporations cut moving benefits. In 1971, an average of $3,539 was paid in employee moving benefits. By 1973 that was reduced to $2,994 (Upson, 1974).

The New York Times reported that in 1973, 37% of 300 client corporations had some refusals and by 1974, 57% refused to move (Vecsey, 1975). Nation's Business reported that ten times more executives refused transfers in 1975 than 1974 (Costello, 1976). U.S. News and World Report wrote that fewer people moved in 1977 of any year since record keeping began on mobility in 1948 (1977). Foegen (1977) reported that 42% of employees were saying "no" to moves and that 46% of wives were now in the workplace.

The women's movement resulted in women having a stronger voice in moving decisions. Some were now seeking careers which, were being hindered by their husbands' frequent relocations. This gradual change in women's roles from silent partner to equal partner may have also played a part in the refusal of transfers in the 70s.

Dual-Careers in the 70s

Another change was taking place in how women viewed work. Seidenberg said that the earlier view was that women believed they could only attain financial success through a man, either a husband or doting father. According to Fuchs, women's work was viewed as a "bridging function between school and marriage," (1971, p. 497) therefore, training should not last too long or be too expensive. Women had always worked out of economic need with a small percentage considered *professionals.* Early into the 70s corporations were discovering that women were entering into more professional careers than in the past and that they would soon be dealing with dual-career couples when relocating (Business Week, 1972).

Dual-Careers and Relocation

Rapoport and Rapoport (1971) discussed dual-careers and relocation. They said that the lack of freedom to relocate was an obstacle to upward mobility and often a source of frustration to the career minded. A career, as opposed to a job, involved commitment and had a continuous developmental character. Foster and Liebrenz said this brought to the forefront many of the problems in relocation and when a "woman redefines herself as a legitimate human being" (1977, p. 71) she is no longer willing to pay the psychic costs of building a new identity or career in each location. Whose career would take precedence was now an issue that couples would have to discuss, as more and more fit the category of dual-career.

Rapoport and Rapoport said that frequently marriages had hidden contracts. A common one was the explicit statement "I want you to do whatever makes you happy." The other implicit part of the statement was "as long as it doesn't affect your attending to my needs" (1971, p. 18). They found that the wife still carried a larger portion of the household and childcare needs of the family even when both had careers. In addition, more wives moved for their husbands' careers than vice-versa. Husbands were perceived as not being serious about their career if they moved for their wife. Moreover, men said that women received sympathy and support when they moved for their husband's career. When a man moved for his wife, he received scorn.

In 1976 only 5% to 10% of relocated employees were female (Todd, 1994). These numbers would show an increase in future decades but companies would continue to relocate more male employees.

The Rapoports were among the first to predict that dual-careers would continue to increase and that this would have widespread social effects. They believed that not only would this affect how society viewed women's work roles outside the family, but it would mean a more symmetrical power structure within the family system.

Quality of Life

Corporations that believed only financial considerations were involved when employees refused to move were surprised to learn that the major reason being given was quality of life (Gilliland, 1979; Kanter, 1977; Maynard & Zawacki, 1979). This would prove to be a major factor in future relocation decisions.

In their search for self-fulfillment, families of the 70s wanted to take time "To stop and smell the flowers" ('Mobile society...', Time, 1978, p. 73). Some thought that this quality of life could best be achieved in smaller communities. A new trend emerged of moving to small towns instead of big cities. 1.7 million more people moved from the cities rather than into them and rural areas began growing faster than urban areas (Time, 1976). Not only were the mobility rates beginning to decline but the migration patterns were changing as well. The desire to live in more rural areas could not always be achieved, especially now with two careers to consider. DeJong reported in 1977 that 76% in his sample preferred a rural area but 58% of these relocated to a city or suburb.

For the first time employees began to challenge the corporations. Now it was not only if and when, but where they would transfer. The generation that had questioned Vietnam was now questioning where their loyalty lay – to the corporation, or to themselves and their families.

Edstrom and Galbraith (1977) mentioned loyalty to the corporation as being reinforced by relocation. It may be that transfers serve to reinforce one's loyalty if one's perception was that one benefited from the move. Pinder (1989) believed that loyalty to the corporation was damaged by relocation because of the disruption to the family. He also reported a greater satisfaction among employees who had requested the relocation than in those who had been requested to relocate. It may also be that if the transfers are not perceived by the family to be beneficial and are not undertaken voluntarily, it may serve to alienate the family from the corporation.

Studies on Children in the 70s

Whalen and Fried (1973) studied geographic mobility and student achievement. They found conflicting results in the studies they examined. Because of this they concluded, "mobility was too broad a variable to test independently" (p. 163). They agreed with Gilliland (1967) who had suggested that one should take into account I.Q. and socioeconomic level. When using these variables in their study they were able to conclude that mobility benefited students of high intelligence but had a negative impact on students of low intelligence. This concurred with Gilliland's earlier study.

Shaw and Pangman in a study of military children following a move concluded that while there were instances of a move having "an adverse effect on the emotional well-being of children" (1975, p. 416), the family move in and of itself "was neither intrinsically pathogenic or stressful" (ibid.).

Shaw and Pangman believed that children might be vulnerable at particular developmental stages. For example, a move may upset the delicate balance of early school children in the process of resolving separation conflicts and adjusting to new authority figures. Moreover, young adolescents, who are struggling to separate themselves from their parents, depend on their peer group at this time. When separated from that support they may find difficulty achieving successful resolution of this stage.

Shaw, in a later study on overseas military adolescents, found them particularly vulnerable at this stage. Adolescence is the second individuation stage and a family move at this time may leave the child with "an impoverished sense of self-esteem and trust in his capacity for autonomy and self-direction" (1979, p. 197).

Werkman agreed that adolescence was the most vulnerable stage to move a child. He believed that highly mobile adolescents were at high risk for developing problems "involving self-image, views of the future, and their ability to make new intimate relationships with others" (1979, p. 176).

Tooley (1970) found two age groups of children to be particularly vulnerable when moving. First, she listed young adolescents, 13 and 14 year olds whom she believed missed their peer relationships and needed them to help successfully transition to adulthood. Second, were six-year-olds or first graders who were in the process of transferring their allegiance from home to school. Both groups, Tooley believed, were already in a delicate developmental stage which moving could upset. Tooley suggested that if problems should arise, brief psychotherapy or family counseling was an appropriate intervention.

Margolis (1979) said that many families in her study had a child whom they would describe as a loner, but they could remember a time several moves before when that child had many friends. She attributed it to a succession of moves.

It may be that the timing of a move in a child's life is a critical factor in their adjustment. Many researchers appear to believe that adolescence is the most difficult stage to move a child. This was followed by preschoolers, and some cited nine and ten year olds. It should also be remembered that nine and ten years olds are at the age when one makes *best friends*. If one interrupts this stage, it is possible that the hurt of leaving a best friend will discourage a child from making another. On the other hand, if this stage is interrupted, a child may not experience having a best friend and subsequent relationships may be more superficial. Parents could be made more aware of what their children need at different developmental stages.

Schaller (1975) in a study of German school children found that the children's greatest concern was leaving their old friends and making new ones. In addition, he found that children, especially boys in grades four and five, are sometimes hostile to newcomers and that this could be a difficult time for children to move. Schaller believed that geographic mobility was related to poor school adjustment and poor peer relationships. He also believed, in contrast to Whalen and Fried's 1973 U.S. study, that high socioeconomic level and high mobility was the least favorable combination. Cultural differences should always be taken into account when evaluating studies and may account for the conflicting results.

Studies Showing Favorable Results

Tooley studied the adjustment problems of families related to mobility. Tooley believed that moving is such a common phenomena that mobility related problems are frequently overlooked and, "that conceptualizing the move as a pivotal incident greatly facilitated diagnostic assessment of family and individual dynamics and helped focus treatment plans" (1970, p. 378). She concluded that moving seemed to improve family adjustment almost as often as it disturbed it and was reluctant to define it as a stressor.

Upson believed that transfers enriched the family by "expanding horizons, breeding poise and understanding, knitting cohesiveness in families and giving invaluable lessons in geography, social mores, personalities and behavior" (1974, p. 78).

Mann (1972) found that high mobile college students experienced less anxiety and adapted better to college life than their low mobile counterparts.

Some studies, mentioned earlier as reporting negative findings, such as Weissman and Paykel also mentioned that "moving can be beneficial" (1972, p. 24). The full quote reads "while moving can be beneficial, it can mean multiple losses to the individual" (ibid.) and they go on to say that it is the losses that lead to depression. Still, they concede that moving can be beneficial. Gaylord also concedes while mentioning many negative aspects to relocation that "for some, moving can be a blessing rather than a burden" (1979, p. 187).

Glueck was quoted as suggesting that there is a "general absence of problems in corporate families subject to geographic relocation" (Richards, Donohue, & Gullotta, 1985, p. 63). Glueck evaluated Veiga's 1972 study of 1,000 Midwest executives who were generally favorable about transfers for career advancement. The executives also believed that their children were not "appreciably" affected by the move, and that their wives were only "moderately affected by the changes" (Glueck, 1974, p. 69).

Glueck said that he spoke to some of the wives following the moves and that "rarely is their evaluation as positive" (ibid.). In addition, Glueck said, "excessive mobility exists now" (ibid.) and the ones bearing the costs of this mobility were the "wives and children without close friends and communities lacking local leadership because of frequently transferred managers" (ibid.).

Margolis (1979) also mentioned the studies showing favorable results. She found three problems with them. First, that they are frequently sponsored by companies that initiate transfers; second, that executives and their wives tend to deny their problems; third, that the studies frequently use questionnaires which cannot really evaluate the complexity of a relocation.

One such study by Jones, done with a grant from Allied Van Lines, summarized the responses of 256 women to a questionnaire. Jones found them to be generally "happy with the new community and with the personality changes that have occurred as a result of their moving experiences" (1973, p. 210). She does say that there is "indication of severe strain at specific stages in the moving process" (ibid., p. 217) and that it was more pronounced in certain categories. For example, Jones reported that women in the

40 to 49 age group cried more frequently during moving and that women with less formal education reported feeling more lonely and detached from others during moving.

Another study in this category by Barrett and Noble (1973) used questionnaires and was made possible by a grant from Aero-Mayflower Transit Company. Barrett and Noble reported, "The results of this study suggest that anxiety about negative effects of moving on the emotional adjustment of children represented by this sample are largely unfounded" (1973, p. 187). The researchers do say the children sometimes appear disturbed following the move but soon return to normal, and that older children have more difficulty than younger children making new friends. They believed however, that any environmental change could precipitate a problem and that "the long distance move should be laid to rest as a specific variable in children's disorders" (ibid., p. 188).

Finally, the Employee Relocation Council (ERC)[3] sponsored a study by Herman[4] and Werbel on the effects of job transfer on employees and their families.

[3] The ERC describes itself as " a professional membership organization of corporations concerned with employee transfer. The Council is composed of approximately 1,000 major U.S. and multi-national corporations, as well as all the major national relocation management companies. ERC also has more than 8,000 associate and affiliate members representing appraisers, real estate brokerage firms, the moving industry and other specialized relocation service businesses." (Cetron, Lucken, McFadden, & Weir, 1987, Preface).

[4] Jeanne Brett Herman a.k.a. Jeanne Brett, Professor of Dispute Resolution and Organizations at the J. L. Kellogg Graduate School of Management, Northwestern University.

This *Baseline Survey* [5] says "it dispels a number of the apparent misconceptions about the impact of employee mobility" (Herman & Werbel, 1978, Introduction). In addition, that a majority of employees were generally satisfied with their companies' relocation policies, believed that moving provided opportunities for career advancement, and said they would move again.

However, over a third of the families reported that the last move was *difficult* or *very difficult.*

> The women, themselves, experienced problems leaving old friends and having to be separated from their husbands. Their children, especially the teenagers, experienced problems leaving old friends, making new friends and with school. Children who had finished school, but were still living at home, had a particularly difficult time adjusting to the move. (ibid., p. 17)

Overall, the report served to reinforce the belief that moving could be difficult for some and, if there was an emotional price to be paid, it was the wives and children who were paying it.

Discussion

Toffler, Seidenberg, and Packard may have helped set the negative tone and direction of the research in this decade. The focus of studies was on depression, isolation, stress, and the *problem* of mobility and its effect on children and the family.

It is important to note that many of the negative studies

[5] The preliminary Baseline Survey was published in 1978. The final report was published in 1980 and comments on the final report will be discussed in Chapter VII, The 80s.

were on clinical, military, or non-American populations. Many who read Toffler, Packard, or Seidenberg were not aware of the differences in populations and may have been left with the impression that everyone who moved in corporate America faced dire consequences. Many families did experience problems, but many families appeared to move successfully. The important part that these authors played in the research was that for the first time the studies looked at the corporate lifestyle and its effects on the family. The resulting studies appeared to indicate that there were risks for several family members. Women could be at risk for depression, and men could be at increased risk of heart attacks from stress. Children were shown to be at the greatest risk when moved at certain vulnerable developmental stages. Most agreed that these stages were adolescence, followed by preschoolers.

In addition, there were indications that a succession of moves could bring about changes in the family system. Not only might the family system become more tightly closed putting the family at risk if a crisis occurred, but also the family might not be developing close long lasting and satisfying friendships outside of the family. A closed nuclear family might find it difficult to meet all of the intimacy and friendship needs of its members.

The negative reports caused many corporate families to question their mobile lifestyle. By mid-decade the negative reports, combined with a recession, caused a drop in corporate mobility. In order to entice families to move the corporations began offering more generous and flexible moving packages.

While no longer as loyal to the corporation, families remained committed to their careers and their belief in the *efficacy of mobility*. Their value systems had incorporated the belief that mobility was good for their careers. Just how voluntary these moves were remains a question, for the belief also remained strong that one cannot turn down a transfer without detrimental effects on one's career. Burke (1974) found that 83% of the employees he surveyed believed this.

In the 80s, families themselves will continue to struggle with the question of how to balance work and family needs. In relocation sometimes the needs of one family member must be weighed against the needs of the entire family. The change in the moving patterns from cities to small towns and rural areas may, in fact, have been an attempt to meet these needs. A place where both careers and the family might flourish; a community where one is known and feels a sense of belonging; the Gemeinschaft ideal. This generation of corporate families had brought their values with them to corporate America and the corporations were learning to deal with them.

As corporate mobility moves into the 80s researchers continue to look at and study the risk factors for the family. Relocation becomes more complex as dual-career numbers increase and eldercare and daycare issues become mobility concerns for the *sandwich generation.* This generation will be the first to try incorporating two careers, children, and elderly parents, into a mobile lifestyle. It will prove overwhelming for some, but others will see themselves as trailblazers and find unique solutions hoping others will follow.

CHAPTER VII

THE 80s / THE NEW PIONEERS

It looms as the omnipotent giver and taker of quality of life - The Company. It can play the indulgent father and bestow bonuses, cars, trips, or it can divide families and send them scrambling in search of psychological bandages. Like a grand puppeteer, it can manipulate the strings of its employees' futures and dance them across the years or cut them and drop those dangling lives into a heap [1]

The 80s opened on a high note with the release of the American hostages by Iran. The symbolic yellow ribbons worn for the hostages were put away, but during the decade America would face many challenges.

Terrorists bombed commercial airliners and attacked Americans worldwide. The U.S. not only reached the brink of war with Libya and invaded Panama, but also engaged in a brief war in Granada.

At home, the country was in a recession and there was high unemployment. Homelessness became a major issue, and it was clear that the dream of social justice for all was not yet a reality. In contrast, Wall Street was booming and the word *yuppie* was coined for the young upwardly mobile

[1] Denise V. Lang "The Phantom Spouse/ Helping You and Your Family Survive Business Travel or Relocation" 1988, p. 7.

professionals rising fast in the business world. Drug use was reported high on Wall Street and Main Street. A frightening and incurable viral disease began to spread that was finally given a name, AIDS. The yellow ribbons that had been worn for the hostages were replaced with red ribbons for the victims of AIDS as the disease took its toll.

While America tried to make democracy work at home, the ideal of democracy took hold in Eastern and Western Europe. The cold war slowly began to thaw. By the end of the decade, the world would watch spellbound as East and West Germans together dismantled the most concrete symbol of Communist control, the Berlin Wall. Ironically, as America was struggling to solve its domestic problems the world was embracing democracy.

As formerly Communist countries pioneered their own versions of the American Dream, the families at home, who had been the most ruthless in its pursuit, were beginning to weigh its costs. It was painful for corporate families to admit that the price tag for pursuing the American Dream might be depression, stress, and troubled families. Now, as housing prices fell, their financial rewards might be in jeopardy as well. Transferees were reluctant to accept losses on their current homes and reinvest at new locations with financing costs at peak levels.

At the same time the number of women in the workforce continued to increase in skilled professional, technical, and management jobs (see Figure 7).

Figure 7. - The proportion of women working year-round, full-time schedules, selected industries (Axel, 1985, p. 5)

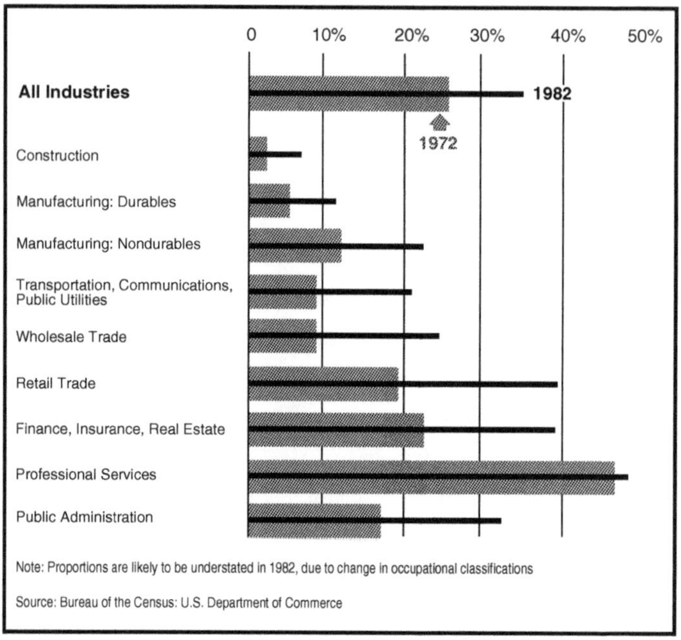

In addition, "from 1978 to 1984, the percentage of women in management positions increased from 10.5% to more than 32%" (Winfield, 1986, p. 33).

Corporate mobility after "nearly a half-decade of flourishing activity came to an abrupt halt" (Kunisch, 1980, p. 25). For the fourth straight year relocation surveys reported that the number of employees willing to relocate had declined (Magnus & Dodd, 1981). From 1980 to 1982, corporate transfers dropped by almost 25% (Winfield, 1986).

Nationwide, mobility continued its slow decline and settled into a rate of between 16.7% and 16.8%; a rate that would continue into the 90s (Hansen, 1996).

Corporations, which had continued to regard relocation as crucial for the employee and the company, slowly began to acknowledge the systems effect taking place. Just as mobility was impacting families, families were impacting mobility. These families would pioneer new family forms in their search to make dual-careers work.

Grief and the Stages of Relocation in the 80s

In the 80s counselors, researchers, and writers of books and articles on relocation continued to apply Kübler-Ross' stages of grief and loss to relocation. Lang (1988), and Nida and Heller (1987), both describe the stages in their books for relocating families. Jones (1984) refers to the stages in her article on coping with relocation stress, as does Skinner (1985). Oglesby (1985) includes them in her study on relocation stress, as do Harrison and Rich in their article on counseling relocating families. Harrison and Rich said, "remarkably similar patterns have been reported for people suffering from disabling injury, rape, divorce, bereavement, immigration, job loss and diagnosis of terminal disease" (1984, p. 24). They also believed that the high stress generated by these events triggered a strong defense mechanism. This served as a protective device until those involved in the event could deal with the reality of the situation. Janik (1988) used the stages in her book on helping families relocate. She said that the denial stage is characterized by a lack of action and the inability to get motivated. Janik also suggested that not meeting one's commitments, thereby angering those whom one is going to leave behind, might be an unconscious way of making the separation easier for some people.

While relocating families may appear to be difficult and unreasonable to those who must deal with them, Harrison and Rich found what the families needed was "time, structure, and compassionate support" (1984, p. 26). When this was provided, the families progressed through the stages at their own pace and their equilibrium was restored.

Handzel and Turici advocated the use of Kübler-Ross' stages in an article for Mobility. They suggested that community colleges might be an appropriate place for courses, workshops, and support groups for relocating families. They said, the stages "may seem overdramatic to those who have never moved, but to those having experienced a transfer, the emotional similarities of the stages are obvious" (1982, p. 12).

In a counseling journal Ramey and Cloud reported that "loneliness, irritability, anger or depression" (1987, p. 155) were all common grief reactions to the losses experienced during relocation. They advocated a model for success with relocation that focused on life skills training that included "decision making, stress management, developing a support system, assertiveness, enhancing positive attitudes and expectations, risk taking, flexibility in thinking and behavior, and assessment of goals, values, and priorities" (ibid., p. 158). They believed that this training could be done in individual, family, or group counseling workshops with the goal of assisting relocating families in achieving the psychological balance essential for a successful relocation.

Depression

Depression remains of interest in the 80s and writers and researchers attempt to understand its relationship to relocation.

The Weissman and Paykel 1972 Yale study on depression in women continues to be cited in the 80s. This study linked depression in women to a recent move, whether the move was voluntary or not. It was cited in Asher (1980), Bayes (1989), Berry (1985), Brett (1982), and Oglesby (1985).

Brett (1982) argued that there was a better model for understanding the connection between relocation and depression in women. Brett did not believe it was the "faulty adaptation to the stresses and changes" promoted by Weissman and Paykel (1972). Nor did she believe Seidenberg's (1973) contention that depression resulted from the inability to rebuild an acceptable identity following relocation. Brett believed that it was the Abramson, Seligman, and Teasdale "learned helplessness model of depression" (1982, p. 452). The model states that "an unwanted transfer may cause depression because the woman believes that if she does nothing about the transfer, it is bound to happen and that there is nothing she can do to keep the transfer from happening" (ibid.).

Kaplan (1983) discussed depression relating to women and what he referred to as *role captivity*. This is where the individual feels obligated to play one role but wishes to play another. The conflict generates stress, which can lead to depression. It is not because the role itself is difficult, but because it is unwanted. While role captivity can apply to men as well as women, Kaplan believed that because women in society have more limited and fixed roles, they were more susceptible.

There are indications that men and women experience relocation differently. Borry (1985), in her book on corporate couples said that she asked two therapists who worked with relocating couples about moving and depression. The male therapist believed that moving acted as a catalyst bringing an existing pathology to the surface. The female therapist said that she believed that the move alone was enough to bring on depression. The therapist said from her own experience following a move she became "a victim to panic, frustration, and depression in an alien environment with no support system" (p. 124).

Others who observed this difference were Imundo (1974) and Renshaw (1976) who referred to this in the previous decade. Now Ammons et al., in their study of upper middle class relocating families, reported finding significant differences in the way that men and women experienced the relocation. "After relocation, women experienced the 'negative' emotions of boredom, loss, depression and loneliness to a significant degree more than men. On the other hand, men experienced enthusiasm significantly more than their wives" (1982, p. 209).

Brett refers to a "learned model of helplessness," Kaplan to role captivity, and Ammons et al. to differences in the way men and women experience relocation. What they may have in common is the way that men and women are socialized in society. Many believe that women are socialized to perceive their roles as less powerful and with fewer choices than men's roles. Schetky discussed how corporate wives were socialized to believe they had no right to be angry about the move when it meant a promotion and raise and this "anger about moves was especially difficult for wives to handle" (1982, p. 867). The wife felt powerless to object and did not want to be blamed for ruining their husband's career. Companies say officially that they do not penalize employees who do not transfer. However, the unofficial norms of the companies say otherwise (Pinder, 1989). Socialization may cause wives to react in a way that they think society expects, not how they want to. Unexpressed anger, turned inward, can lead to depression.

The career wife who leaves her job to follow her

husband's career may also be reacting to socialization. Society has long held the belief that the husband's work role should dominate relocation decisions. Therefore, she does what she thinks she should do, not what she wants to do. A man who moves for his wife's career may also be at risk, and there are indications that men receive less societal support for this decision. However, it may be that men will express this anger outwardly and it may not lead to depression.

Not everyone may feel anger, but if it is not recognized, or it is denied and turned inward, it could be one of the reasons for the depression associated with relocation.

Social Networks and Social Support

Loneliness has also been linked to depression (McKain 1973; Vandervelde, 1979: Weiss, in Caplan & Killilea, 1976). Ramey and Cloud (1987) distinguished between types of loneliness. The loneliness associated with a relocation, according to Ramey and Cloud, was situational and would be solved when one found friends in the new location. It could, however, develop into chronic loneliness if one is not able to develop lasting relationships over a period of years.

This type of isolation is similar to the social isolation referred to by Weiss (1973) in the previous chapter. Weiss said that social isolation was dependent on friends, neighbors, and kinfolk. Emotional isolation occurred when one lost a significant relationship such as the intimate tie of a spouse, parent, or child. Ramey and Cloud (1987) did not refer to the presence of a significant other, but the chronic loneliness they referred to might be similar to the emotional isolation described by Weiss (1973).

Writers and researchers frequently refer to the loss of social networks and social support when one relocates. In relocation, having a viable social support network is believed to mitigate the stress, and assist the family members in adapting to the new environment (Carter, 1981; Hendershott, 1989). In the previous decade (Brown, Bhrolchain, & Harris, 1975) found, that in working with clinical populations, social support served as a buffer for life stress including depression.

Earlier writers claimed that extended families would be virtually destroyed by mobility. McCubbin and Boss reported that the previous decade's work on stress and coping revealed that "kinship systems are alive and well, and play a major role in supporting families under stress" (1980, p. 429).

The terms social network and social support, while related, have different meanings. Walker, MacBride, and Vachon defined an individual's social network as "that set of personal contacts through which the individual maintains his social identity and receives emotional support, material aid and services, information, and new social contacts" (1977, p. 35). According to Lin, Dean, and Ensel (1981) the network is the structural framework through which the individual is able to receive support. However, being embedded in a network does not guarantee that one will be supported. It is the quality of the relationships that one has within the network that determines this.

Social support refers to the recognition and knowing that one is supported by others. "The amount of help received is not always related to perceptions of being supported" (Liem & Liem, in Kaplan, 1983, p. 143).

The social network, then, is the framework, and social support is the feeling of being supported that is achieved if one is able to access support from the network. The role of social support for individuals and families in making them less vulnerable in a crisis is well documented (Caplan & Killilea, 1976; Kaplan, 1983; McCubbin, Dahl, Lester, Benson, & Robertson, 1976; McCubbin, Joy, Cauble, Comeau, Patterson, & Needle, 1980).

Social support has been cited previously as a factor in relocation. Now, Ramey and Cloud say, "the knowledge of an existing and available support network influences an individual's perception of distress and his or her assessment of ability to cope" (1987, p. 152). The feeling of being supported may contribute to the family's ability to recover from the stress or crisis state and assist the family in returning to homeostasis, its pre-move steady state.

There is also evidence that men and women may perceive social support differently. In a study of geographic mobility following divorce, Asher found that "there was a strong tendency for women, particularly non-movers, to base their decision on the presence of a social support system, while men were more concerned with job or school plans" (1980, p. iv). It may also be that the women believed that the marital disruption was enough stress in their lives at the moment and would consider a relocation at a later time.

A Sense of Place

A sense of place and how it is affected by a relocation continues to be mentioned in the 80s. Marc Fried, who in an earlier study connected feelings of grief and loss to a sense of place (in Duhl, 1963), reported on a later study he conducted in 80s. He continued to emphasize the importance of place and said, "the residential environment is a particularly important setting for human behavior by virtue of its significance for roles, relationships, and the sense of place in the world" (1982, p. 107). When people are satisfied in a community, he said it is "the objective features of the residential environment" (ibid.) that account for the satisfaction and that the social interaction is only a minor part of the attachment.

The study of the meaning of place in people's lives and how it is significant to people's ability to function belongs to an area of study called environmental psychology. In explaining this area of study, Rivlin describes a systems perspective. She says there is an "interdependence of people with the place in which they live, recognition that people and places are not independent parts" (1982, p. 77). Rivlin further explains that moves are more than disruption and effort. They are filled with emotion, as complex social networks are uprooted along with the layers of memories that this setting holds for the people involved. She sees the environment as an organizing frame, a canvas on which these experiences have taken place. The memories of these are the "invisible glue attaching people to the setting" (ibid.). This may account for why we are drawn to a setting long after the people have left and even after a house may no longer be standing.

How place helps define identity is complex. For some, the place may help define a role, such as a classroom to a student or a hospital to a nurse. There also may be defining qualities for the person, not only as an individual, but also as a member of a larger group. For example, the classroom may have helped the child learn who they were in terms of their strengths and weaknesses but it may have also socialized them into their larger peer group, a crowd of friends, or the entire school. Whether one has lived "in a slum or an affluent suburb, the country or an urban area, each of these contributes special qualities to the residents' personal functioning and to that essence of individuality that we call the self" (ibid., p. 80).

Ramey and Cloud state that a "relocation can bring about a change in perception of the person's relationship to the universe and place in relation to the whole" (1987, p. 155).

Nida and Heller, in their book for relocating teenagers, referred to the familiar sense of place as a "mental map" (1987, p. 9) that we have of our old location and how it takes time to form a new one that will restore our comfort level.

Stokols and Shumaker said that the connection of place to health and stress was in the perception of how congruent we were with the place. If we were in a place we disliked for long periods, or we were separated from a place that we wanted to be for long periods, then stress and health problems were more likely to occur. The level of congruence depends on how well the environmental setting meets our needs, which are highly individual and personal.

They found in their research that "increased length of residence does not necessarily promote greater attachment to place and enhanced well-being" (1982, p. 165). This contradicted an earlier study by Kasarda and Janowitz (1974) which had reached that conclusion. By introducing variables not included in the Kasarda and Janowitz study, Stokols and Shumaker found that the "association between length of residence and health was qualified by perceptions of residential choice and congruence, with greater health impairment reported among those who had little choice in moving to their current residence" (1982, p. 165.). They believed that the variables of predictability and control were important in how one perceived the relocation. A forced choice could result in growing animosity toward the new location rather than increased commitment. Stokols and Shumaker believed that while the move itself is often disruptive and stressful it is not inevitably harmful to one's health. They said, "recent demographic data suggest that the majority of mobile Americans change residence voluntarily and without detrimental health consequences" (ibid., p. 152).

Stress and the Family System in the 80s

Stress continues to be discussed in the 80s. Gaylord and Symons said relocation stress is a now recognized phenomenon and the term is used "to refer to all of the normal feelings that can be triggered by a move" (1986, p. 31). That these feelings of anxiety, loss, pain, anger, and isolation might be experienced at various times and degrees by family members. They expressed views similar to earlier researchers who said that the wife pays the greatest price in loss of self esteem and identity, the most difficult ages for relocating children were 3-5 and 14-16, and that more than half of transferred teenagers have personal adjustment problems. The researchers believed that the corporations should provide counseling for the families with educational, therapeutic, and preventative goals to help reduce relocation stress.

Anderson and Stark state, "geographic relocation is well established as a major stress to families" (1988, p. 38) and cite several authors (Brett, 1982; Dransfield, 1984; Hall & Hall in Cooper & Payne, 1980; and Marshall & Cooper, 1976) as agreeing. Anderson and Stark believed that it was repeated moves and involuntary moves that created the most stress in the family system.

Bastress (1986), in her book on spouse relocation said that it has been known for a long time that relocation is one of the most stressful situations that a couple has to deal with. Asher (1980), in her study of geographic relocation following divorce, said that geographic mobility may provide an added stress to an already stressful marriage.

Others believed that it was not the stress alone that was the problem, "it is the denial of stress, however, that is its most damaging aspect" (Holloman, 1985, p. 57).

Ahr referred to a relocation as being emotionally charged and put the "family in the midst of one-third of the primary stressors in contemporary life" (1987, p. 61). Ahr believed that the relocation would not cause a stress reaction if it was not perceived as stressful, or if the families' coping mechanisms were successful. Ahr also believed that the more control the family had over the planning and execution of the relocation, the better they could master the changes the relocation would bring.

Feitler-Karchin and Getting (1987) believed that whether the move was voluntary or not affected the level of stress impacting the family.

Hendershott (1989) stated the perception of whether the move was voluntary, and its relation to stress, had to do with the issue of control over one's life. The more choices one had the more perceived control, and the less stress would result. Similar views had been expressed earlier by Renshaw (1976).

In 1983 McCubbin and Patterson published the *double* ABCX model to show how the family reacts to stress. It was based on the original ABCX model developed by Hill in 1949. This new model, for use by clinicians, was developed following research with military families. McCubbin and Patterson found that the family reaction to the impact of a stressor that was perceived as a crisis was determined by multiple factors in interaction with each other. The researchers believed that the kind and number of stressors; the personal, family and community resources; as well as the family's perception of the stressor and their coping behaviors; were all important factors in shaping the ability of the family to adapt to the stressful situation.

McCubbin et al. (1975) said that the closed family system did well in crisis. In this decade, Anderson and Stark quote B. D. Carter as finding "that open laissez-faire families coped better than closed autocratic families, because open families were adept at eliciting needed support" (Carter, 1983, in Anderson & Stark, 1988, p. 38). It appears that the family system may need to be open enough to accept needed support during times of crisis.

The Holmes-Rahe Stress Test also continued in use in the 80s and was recommended for relocating clients by Meltzer and Grandjean, who referred to it in their book on the psychology of moving. They believed that while it identified "some fairly universal problems" (1989, p. 8), the ratings would vary from culture to culture. For example, in some groups a jail term or a baby out of wedlock might be considered commonplace for young adults. In other groups it might mean lifelong shame for the family. Also, because some cultures perceive a large extended family in the same way that other groups perceive the nuclear family, ratings might vary. The perception of the situation determined the level of stress that would impact the family system.

Evans and Bartolomé (1981) in their study of executive stress quote Hans Selye who said, "complete freedom from stress is death" (Selye, in Evans & Bartolomé, 1981, p. 22). The distinction that Selye made was that there is good stress called "eustress" and bad stress called "distress" (ibid.). Both types bring a rush of adrenaline, but "the good stress 'eustress' stimulates body and mind while 'distress' is likelier to produce disease" (ibid., p. 23). "The most severe forms of executive stress, psychologists agree, often are caused by the death of a loved one, a divorce, or a major relocation" (Dunn, 1985, p. 89).

Cetron, Lucken, McFadden, and Weir, in their report on the changing family, said that the new dual-career and non-traditional families were most in need of support when relocating. Many *baby boomers*[2] started their families later

[2] The baby-boom years stretch from 1947 to 1964, a period when a total of 74 million babies were born in the United States. The peak years of the boom, 1957-1961, produced an annual crop of 4.3 million infants–a birth level not reached since, despite the fact that there are more than half again as many women of childbearing age now as in 1960. (Axel, 1985, p. 2).

in order to pursue careers. Today, Cetron et al. said, "the family is no longer an independent unit but an interdependent one. It depends on community-provided support services to meet multi-generational responsibilities" (1987, p. 2). This new "sandwich" (ibid., p. 7) generation is caught in the middle, needing childcare and eldercare for aging parents simultaneously when they move. In addition to these services, after-school programs, housekeeping services, and babysitters for when children are too ill for school, all must be reestablished in the new location. Cetron et al. suggest that companies should incorporate provisions for members of the sandwich generation in their relocation policies. This could include relocating all dependents, which would include aging parents as well as children. They also suggested longer pre-move visits to the new location so that all of these services could be located.

When a wife works outside the home, the family undergoes many changes. Roles are redefined. Husbands frequently help run the household and care for the children. Cetron et al., suggest that the working wife still bears the largest share of the responsibility at home. The family may be better off financially, but relationships can become strained and communication may break down. They also mention that two-earner families lead the nation in divorce.

The distinction should be made here that it is two-earner families, not dual-career specifically, that Cetron et al. is referring to. Two-earner families are defined as one having a career and the other a job. The person with the job generally moves for the person with the career. Traditional women's jobs, sometimes referred to as "pink collar jobs" (ibid., p. 4), are nurses, teachers, bank tellers, store clerks, and secretaries. These jobs are considered transferable, but as women rise in rank and expertise their transferability declines.

Anderson and Stark (1988) said in their article that the families who were most at risk were families that fell into the non-traditional category such as dual-career, single-parent, and stepfamilies. These families, they said, may be confronting many more family issues than traditional families. Dual-career families may be dealing with home/work overload, role ambiguity, and conflicting work demands. Single-parent families may also be dealing with role ambiguity, ongoing litigation issues, downward economic mobility, and loss. Stepfamilies may also be concurrently dealing with ambiguity of roles, ongoing litigation, trying to blend different family histories into one, and emotional issues of loss. From a systems perspective, for all three nontraditional family types, the relocation is "likely to exacerbate the already tenuous family balance" (p. 39).

With non-traditional families growing in number, families may be experiencing even more stress in relocating. The added stress on their family systems may put them in the *at risk* category. The authors suggested transition counseling before and after the move. This would help the individual family members, and the family as a system, develop realistic expectations regarding the relocation.

Researchers and writers continue to build on the work of the previous decades. Some insist that perception is the key as to whether the event will be a stressor or not, and culture is added as a variable. Others say that the key is whether the move is voluntary. Still others refer to the number of stressors as being most important; the pile-up of stress referred to in previous chapters. Support systems continue to be considered an important factor for mitigating stress and the Holmes-Rahe stress test continues in use. There is still interest in executive stress, but new family forms, dual-career families, and non-traditional families become of interest to researchers. While there is no consensus reached, suggestions continue to be made that more support services are needed for the families.

Boss (1980a) discussed stress in the family system and said that all families experience stress from change at various times in their life cycles. This was particularly true when transitioning from one life cycle stage to another.

<u>Life Cycle Stages</u>

Boss (1980a) said that the stress in the family system continues through the transition stage until the system reorganizes and roles are clarified (see Table 2).

Boss' focus was the boundaries of the family system, and she said that as families move through life cycle stages they

Table 2. The stages of the family life cycle

(Carter & McGoldrick 1989, p. 15)

Family Life Cycle Stage	Emotional Process of Transition: Key Principles	Second-Order Changes in Family Status Required to Proceed Developmentally
1. Leaving home: Single young adults	Accepting emotional and financial responsibility for self	a. Differentiation of self in relation to family of origin b. Development of intimate peer relationships c. Establishment of self re work and financial independence
2. The joining of families through marriage: The new couple	Commitment to new system	a. Formation of marital system b. Realignment of relationships with extended families and friends to include spouse
3. Families with young children	Accepting new members into the system	a. Adjusting marital system to make space for children b. Joining in childbearing, financial, and household tasks c. Realignment of relationships with extended family to include parenting and grandparenting roles
4. Families with adolescents	Increasing flexibility of family boundaries to include children's independence and grandparents' frailties	a. Shifting of parent child relationships to permit adolescent to move in and out of system b. Refocus on midlife marital and career issues c. Beginning shift toward joint caring for older generation
5. Launching children and moving on	Accepting a multitude of exits from and entries into the family system	a. Renegotiation of marital system as a dyad b. Development of adult to adult relationships between grown children and their parents c. Realignment of relationships to include in-laws and grandchildren d. Dealing with disabilities and death of parents (grandparents)
6. Families in later life	Accepting the shifting of generational roles	a. Maintaining own and/or couple functioning and interests in face of physiological decline; exploration of new familial and social role options b. Support for a more central role of middle generation c. Making room in the system for the wisdom and experience of the elderly, supporting the older generation without overfunctioning for them d. Dealing with the loss of spouse, siblings, and other peers and preparation for own death. Life review and integration

change members through birth, death, divorce, and remarriage. Until the new boundaries are clarified at all stages of these transition times, and new roles defined, the family will not return to homeostasis, its steady state. The middle stages of the life cycle are characterized,

> by the bearing raising and launching of children during which family resources are at their lowest and pile-up is at its highest. Thus, the middle stages of the family life cycle occur when families are most vulnerable to the stresses of relocation (Brett & Reilly in Robbins, 1992, p. 34)

According to Schetky (1982), statistics indicate that an executive averages four moves between the ages of 35 to 50, which are most often the children's early adolescent and teen years. Not only might the family be dealing with the stress of relocation, but the concurrent stresses of transitioning life cycle stages. This may also have application to dual-career, single-parent, and stepfamilies as they relocate. These families, more than traditional families, will be leaving family members behind. In addition to the normal stress of the relocation, there may be ongoing reorganizing within the family system.

McCubbin and Patterson (1983b) believed that families are in a continuum of adaptation, constantly experiencing changing demands and needs. These occur as the individual family members and the family progress through developmental stages. Demands and needs may also come from outside the immediate family unit, from the extended family, as parents age and need extended care. Need for adaptation may arise from the community, as schools, work, or the neighborhood changes. Finally, society brings change into the family as gender roles change.

The Corporate Family System

The corporate family system was a concern for child psychiatrist Diane Schetky[3]. Her clients were predominantly corporate families and she believed that certain aspects of the lifestyle contributed to the psychopathology she diagnosed in her client families. She described fathers as lacking in empathy, emotionally unavailable, and out of touch with their children's needs. The fathers were often physically absent and psychologically remote. Schetky said there was also role confusion due to the constant entrances and exits of the father. Authority would be delegated to the wife with the father's absence, but, upon return, decisions made by the wife during the absence were often criticized.

The teens had placed "exceedingly high expectations upon themselves, often mirroring parental values" (1982, p. 869). They perceived their fathers as perfect and unapproachable. Schetky believed that many of the children were overindulged and rarely allowed to experience frustration. Their superficial peer relationships and lack of commitment was their way of avoiding pain when the next move came. Some turned to drugs or alcohol, some developed personality disorders, and some, females in

[3] Dr. Schetky is Associate Clinical Professor of Psychiatry, Yale Child Study Center, New Haven, Connecticut.

particular, developed depression, eating disorders. and identity problems. This, Schetky believed, stemmed from the "emphasis placed on outward appearance and pleasing others at the expense of getting to know oneself" (ibid.). Some of the mothers were overly close to their children "making it difficult for the child to separate and individuate" (ibid.).

Gullotta, Stevens, Donohue, and Clark (1981) expressed a similar view and said that corporate families put the needs of the head of the household and the corporation ahead of the individual needs of the children. Schetky found that wives' "physical and emotional dependency on their husbands often led to the need to keep peace at all costs" (1982, p. 868). Thus, when faced with another relocation, the wives did not complain and subordinated their needs to their husbands' careers.

Isolation was also cited as a problem for the families. Sometimes the family was hesitant to get involved in the community, as they knew they would move again, and sometimes the community members, who did not wish to get involved with transients, shunned them. "The net effect of this is to make them cling more to one another and the company" (ibid., p. 863).

In observing corporate family dynamics, Schetky said that one "must look beyond corporations to societal attitudes which foster these conditions. It is quite possible that companies select CEO's who fit this mold because these qualities are self-serving to the companies and are in turn reinforced by the company" (ibid., p. 870). The lack of emotional involvement allows the executive to work long hours and put the company ahead of his family. This served the man's career well, according to Schetky, who quoted a 1982 French study that reported married men outperformed single men, as well as married and single women. Their success was attributed to the fact that these men had supportive wives.

It may be that wives are more willing to move when not invested in a career. Some have suggested that it takes two to maintain a mobile corporate life style and that these wives have chosen to invest in their husbands' careers as the best opportunity for financial security for the family.

Corporate transferees appear to have more traditional families than the general population. In a 1987 survey by Cetron et al. only 39% of corporate spouses worked outside the home. According to a recent Catalyst[4] survey, that is closer to the national average thirty years ago than it is today. "In 1994, 60% of women over 16 in the U.S. were labor force participants, up from 33.9% in 1950" (An HR Timeline, Workforce Magazine On-Line, 1998, p. 1).

"Women have been the dominant component of labor-force growth during the past 30-odd years. For every two men added to the working population since 1950, three women found jobs or were actively seeking work" (Axel,

[4] Catalyst is a New York City based, independent, not-for-profit organization founded in 1962 to enable women in business and the professions achieve their maximum potential and to help employers capitalize on the talents of their female employees.

1985, p. 2).

Figure 8 illustrates the dramatic rise of women in the work force in recent years.

Figure 8. - Narrowing the gender gap in the labor force
(Axel, 1985, p. 3)

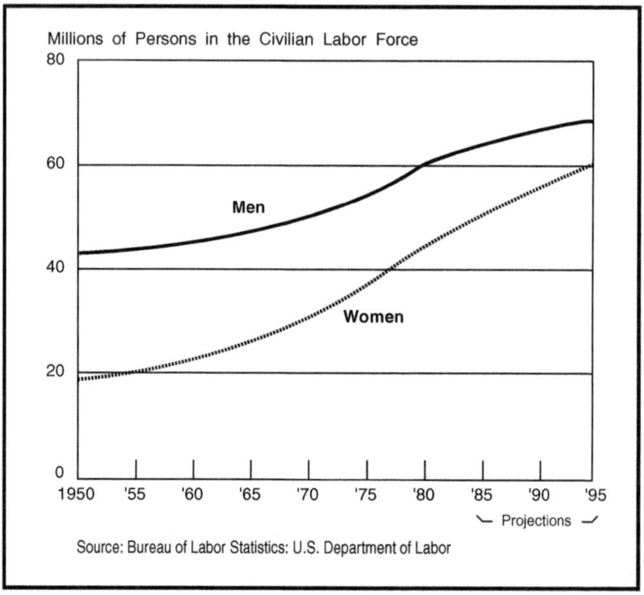

The numbers of women entering careers continue to grow in the general population. If the numbers continue to increase in the corporate population as well, relocation may become increasingly difficult for corporate couples.

According to Schetky these qualities of highly authoritarian father, high incidence of behavior disorders among children, isolation, and lack of support also have been described in military families. She believed it would be interesting to study well functioning corporate families as well as affluent families who were not mobile.

It should be stressed that the pathology described was in the families seeking treatment not in the entire mobile corporate population.

Gullotta and Donohue said that corporate couples share the "common values of hard work, efficiency, competency, and loyalty, and this forms the basis of an unspoken business contract as well as a marriage contract" (1981b, p. 152). They found that as the husband climbs the corporate ladder and gains in status, he shares his work less and less with his wife. The wife, in turn, is occupied as homemaker, but her contribution is less valued in the eyes of the family. Finally, what results are new marriages, the husband to the corporation and the wife to the family.

For the family seeking treatment, the authors, both family therapists, said that they found conventional family therapy approaches did not work well with corporate families. The authors stress that, despite any problems, the family is deeply invested in and committed to the lifestyle. Once out of conventional treatment the families return to their old behaviors. They described the corporate family as "constantly stressed yet generally quite stable, and unique in terms of style and structure" (ibid., p. 154). There are frequent exits and entrances, high socioeconomic status, and long and intense work hours. The wife is usually the one to express the pain in the family, and from a systems view she is expressing the pain for the whole family system. The approach the authors find effective is to identify the familiar and possibly unique coping styles of each family which have worked in the past. They then build on those coping styles attempting to restore stability to the family.

Their approach sounds to be what would be described today as *Brief Solution Focused Therapy*.

The Myth of Separate Worlds

Kanter (1977) and Piotrkowski (1979) first discussed the myth of separate worlds in the previous decade. Now, Voydanoff says, "There is a growing interest in examining the impact of executive work roles on corporate families in spite of a general tendency on the part of corporations and executives to ignore or deny the relatedness of work and family roles" (1980, p. 489). She said that successful executives frequently develop personality traits that are inconsistent with successful family life, "that managerial careers stress the development of the head at the expense of the heart" (ibid., p. 491).

Evans and Bartolomé also believed that there was an interchange of energy between the worlds of work and family which they referred to as "emotional spillover" (1981, p. 16). They believed that it is mostly one-way with a negative impact of stress from work to family. They said they found executives were better at switching off home problems when at work than they were at switching off work problems when at home. When the stress came home, it impacted the whole family system.

Berry, in her book on corporate couples, devoted a whole chapter to what she called *stress and spillover*. She defined spillover as the effect that "the employment of one or both of the marriage partners has on their lives outside of the workplace" (1985, p. 173). She said that corporations deny the existence of spillover and say they could not inquire as "it would intrude on the private lives of our employees" (ibid.). Berry also mentions how societal roles are changing and that researchers "have used traditional work/home standards – blue-collar, agricultural, and private employment – to analyze a nontraditional work/home lifestyle – corporate employment" (ibid., p. 174). She sees the transient, mobile corporate family as a system with the spillover stress affecting everyone in the system. Mental spillover can be destructive, she said, because when employees are preoccupied with work at home and "psychologically unavailable" (ibid., p.176) they hear but do not listen. Spillover impacts the marriage and family relationships. Berry also believed that there was more stress brought home from work than brought to work from home. Voles mentions that "many corporations say they do not feel that it is their place to become involved in family matters" (1982, p. 73). Apparently, the myth of separate worlds was alive and well in the 80s.

Dual-Careers in the 80s

Early Socialization

Christine Wilson, the Managing Editor of Mobility, reported in 1985 that "more than 60% of married couples have dual careers and by the 90s it is expected to increase to well over 80%" (p. 93). She predicted that professional careers for women would increase as over 50% were currently undergraduates, 37% were in law school, and 33% were MBA candidates. In addition, 52% of these families needed the second income to purchase a home. Home ownership, which had been considered possible in earlier decades, was becoming unattainable as housing costs soared out of proportion to income (see Figure 9).

Figure 9. - Housing costs in proportion to income

(Graph created from data in 'An HR Timeline', 2/98)

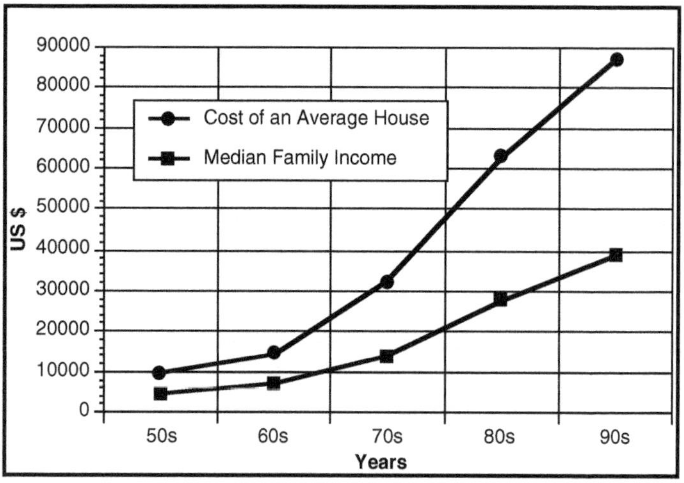

Clearly, both were factors in the changing workplace, women were entering professional careers and many families needed that second income to buy housing. A Catalyst survey disclosed that the women who were entering the workforce at this time were committed to their work and had defined career paths (Wilson, 1985). According to Regan, researchers had taken for granted the assumption that, "women work for social reasons and men work for power, prestige, and achievement" (1985, p. 986).

Regan's 1985 study concluded that women now "expected to gain life satisfaction from the professional rewards of money, power, leadership, prestige and esteem" (ibid., p. 989). The conflict, Regan said, was that "society continues to reward values of assertiveness, egoism, and independence while conditioning women for passive nurturing roles at home and in the semi-professional workplace. Thus, women's socialization reinforces the incompatibility of career and family" (ibid., p. 990).

Houseknecht and Macke (1981) believed that when both spouses were competing in the work arena there was pressure on one to fill the nurturer role. Because of women's socialization, there would be more pressure on the woman fill the nurturer role. They argued that this could result in lowered career aspirations for women or their conscious rejection of parenthood. It may also make the family a source of stress rather than comfort and make the dual-career lifestyle difficult to maintain.

Rapoport and Rapoport (1978) who coined the term *dual-career*, and conducted extensive research on dual-career British couples, believed that part of the resistance on the part of society in accepting a dual-career lifestyle is that it runs counter to traditional cultural family norms. They said that there is voiced support, but that internalized values from early socialization produces anxiety, tension, and guilt. Heckman, Bryson, and Bryson (1977) shared this view. They added that one of the most frequently cited problems expressed by dual-career couples was the expectation on the part of others that the dual-career couple conform to traditional male and female roles.

Socialization also appears to have an impact on the dual-career couples themselves. Over 50% of wives were willing to relocate and find a new job if their husbands received a satisfactory offer, but only 25% of the wives expected their husbands to do the same for them (Wallston, Foster & Berger, 1978, p. 11).

A study by Gilliland of thirteen dual-career couples indicated only a slightly higher percentage of reluctance on the part of the husbands to relocate for their wives. In five of the thirteen couples, "the wife was willing to move without conditions, while the husband was either not willing or only with good prospects" (1979, p. 352). Moreover, in three couples the situation was reversed, and in the remaining five couples, the couples gave equal consideration to each others career. Gilliland concluded that there were tradeoffs necessary in order to maintain a dual-career lifestyle. This "new set of values included priority to self, the marriage relationship, and a way of life that provides material and non-material rewards" (ibid., p. 357).

Keith and Schafer (1980) said that two full-time working parents is still an innovative form, and that during periods of role transition and change, society engages in more questioning than when the pattern is well established. They added that one method of adaptation, when both work, is for husbands to become more involved in household tasks. However, Keith and Schafer reported that men experienced more stress when doing tasks normally expected of women and that women may feel guilty when men help. Keith and Schafer believed that "both sexes may be somewhat disadvantaged by traditional attitudes" (1980, p. 483).

The Rapoports also reported on societal pressure in their 1978 review of dual-career literature. They quoted a 1977 London Times article discussing the increase in juvenile delinquency; "One factor is the parent-child relationship, as a result of the increasing number of mothers who take up full time employment" (Krebs, 1977 in Rapoport & Rapoport, 1978, p. 9). They said that Professor Krebs cited British psychiatrist John Bowlby who attached great importance to early mothering and that Krebs implied, but did not actually advocate, a return to traditional family patterns with mother at home. This is consistent with an earlier (1971) article by Rapoport and Rapoport in which they suggested that if the dual-career couple chose not to have children they were considered "odd, or at best, unfortunate" (1971, p. 527). They implied that the source of the anxiety and doubts were clear and that it was simply that people were socialized in norms and values, which were now thirty years old, but still persisted. Frequently, the dual-career couple espouses equality. During times of crisis, however, they may revert to earlier socialization of more traditional values rather than look for innovative and creative solutions.

Kilpatrick (1982) points out that extended family and friends, who are the usual support system, may in fact exert the most pressure on the dual-career couple to become more traditional. More useful, she says, is letting them know that they are not alone in trying to make a two career family work. It has been done successfully by others, so share with them how other couples in their situation have resolved similar issues.

Stress and Dual-Career

Corporations, now aware of the dual-career trend, wanted to determine the consequences of dual-careers on corporate mobility. However, the surprising fact reported by Crosby in a 1985 survey of Fortune 500 companies was that 20 out of 28 companies did not even know how many of their employees were dual-career. Clearly, this is one of the consequences for the family if corporations continue to subscribe to the myth of separate worlds. If the corporations did not know how many couples were dual-career, then they obviously had no idea how many of their employees faced the additional stresses that dual-career couples face when relocating.

There is the stress of trying to protect a double income and the stress of maintaining the psychological commitment to both careers, which is added to the normal stresses that the relocation brings to the family (Magnus & Dodd, 1981). Crosby (1985) believed that the impact of the relocation brought stress to the whole family, and especially the transferee's spouse, whose career could be jeopardized by the relocation[5].

Shahnasarian (1989) believed that dual-career needs and psychological needs were interrelated when relocating. He believed that the biggest source of stress during the move was financial, as the pressure was on the relocated spouse to regain income quickly so that the couple could resume their pre-move lifestyle. This was often at a time when the spouse had ambivalent feelings over leaving and anxiety over a job search. The employed spouse is often less available to help at home and for emotional support because of the added job responsibilities that come with starting a new job. If there are children who are having trouble adjusting to the move, the combination of emotional, psychological, and relationship factors have a reciprocal effect on each other, and will result in stress on the family system. He suggested

[5] Traditionally, the relocating spouse was female. By 1985, 10% were male with the figure slowly increasing (Wilson, 1985).

that organizations initiating the relocation offer outside career and emotional counseling to help support the family.

One of the most common sources of stress facing dual-career couples is work and role overload. Skinner discussed this in her 1980 review of dual-career literature. She said that much of the literature suggests that "stress is inherent in a dual-career lifestyle" (p. 473). Yet, she believed that part of the pressure was coming from the fact that it was a "relatively new and minority pattern" (ibid.). As such, dual-career couples feel that they must come up with individual solutions without outside support. Skinner mentioned the Rapoports 1978 study, which suggested that work overload was affected by conditions which were, in part, self-imposed. Domestic overload is common, as chores at home must be handled after the workday, children are often present, and living standards are high. According to Bryson and Bryson (1978), the majority of home responsibilities fall to the wife, so that she winds up with two careers; home and family; and her outside work.

Additional strains could arise if there were personal conflicts in the early gender role socialization and current practice. Despite its growing prevalence, the dual-career marriage is still considered different from society's norms and the couple may experience stress and feel pressure to conform. There may also be stress when the life cycle stage of the family conflicts with career demands. Researchers suggested that older professional couples or childless couples found the lifestyle easier to negotiate. Many researchers stated that younger dual-career couples with children reported strain associated with childcare arrangements, especially the women.

Another possible source of strain may arise after the move. Veiga in his study of two thousand managers reported some surprising findings. Apparently, many employees were lead to believe that their moves were promotions, when in fact they were lateral moves. Employees reported that "85% of their moves were upward, 12% lateral and 3% downward" (1981, p. 21). Average corporate estimates were "40% upward, 51% lateral and 9% downward" (ibid.). Veiga said "organizations tend to cloak demotions in a good deal of ambiguity" (ibid.) so that it was difficult for employees to see a demotion or lateral move for what it was.

If a dual-career couple has relocated for what the transferred employee perceived to be a promotion, and then discovers it was really a lateral move, then two careers have been affected. This may cause the stress level, which before may have been manageable, to rise to crisis level for the family system.

Relocation and Dual-Career

Holmstrom (1972) reported that about 75% of dual-career couples are faced with the issue of geographic mobility in order to advance their careers. There are many reasons. In establishing two careers, it is frequently difficult to find an organization simultaneously seeking to fill two positions that would be a perfect fit for the couple; and even in the event this occurred, that would be willing to hire husband and wife. Anti-nepotism rules still exist in many work environments. When considering choices, one spouse may have to leave a valued career position and look for work in the new area. They may find themselves in a market in which they are either underemployed or unemployed.

Kilpatrick, who examined relocation and dual-career families, viewed the relocation in terms of crisis theory. She said, that when viewing the family as a system, all family members are interdependent, and so change in one member affects the entire system. Crises can occur, Kilpatrick says, when the dual-career couple "seeks to maintain a family life when none of the usual family roles are completely delegated or abrogated" (1982, p. 363).

For example, there are frequently hidden contracts in marriages and many involve roles. In relocation, the wife may follow the husband on the first move. His assumption may then be that she will continue to do this. Hers may be that he will follow her on the next move. The roles were not clearly defined. The expectations of each partner will define the next relocation as opportunity or crisis.

Traditionally, American couples have located where the husbands have jobs (Long, 1974). When relocating,

Kilpatrick said, the husband's career was traditionally viewed as more important. The wife followed the husband from job to job and "generally made the greater sacrifices in regard to her own career, by either not working, taking a series of dead end jobs, or starting over in every new location" (1982, p. 364). Both husbands and wives expressed this view when asked whose job dominated moving decisions (Bird & Bird, 1985).

In a study of couples where both were completing Ph.D. degrees, most of the sample espoused egalitarian decision making. However, when the time for the actual move took place, they generally moved to the husband's job location (Wallston et al., 1978). The authors suggested that *institutional constraints*[6] were partly responsible for traditional job decisions. For example, a university or corporation might have a policy against hiring the spouse of an employee. In addition, some researchers have mentioned that there are careers that are extremely demanding and require a support person. This causes stress on, and is incompatible with, a dual-career lifestyle.

According to Anderson and Stark (1988), the moving patterns of most dual-career couples differ from that of traditional families. Employees are less likely to relocate when their spouses are employed. This is particularly true when the spouse is highly paid and the potential move is to a small town. When dual-career couples relocate, they may desire small town life, but they tend to move to metropolitan

[6] a.k.a. – Anti-Nepotism personnel policies.

areas large enough for both to find employment. The feeling is that a woman is less likely to initiate a family move to further her career, "but may be able to prevent a family move to maintain employment continuity" (Shaklee, 1989, p. 729). Shaklee believes that it is not actually gender that is controlling the moving decision, but money. Studies of actual moving patterns are done, said Shaklee, in a non-egalitarian working world where men are paid better then women. It may be that as more women enter professional careers, the egalitarian ideal espoused by the graduating students will come to pass.

Commuter Marriage

Rather than giving one career priority over the other, a solution that some dual-career couples consider is the commuter marriage. This is an emerging form in which the marriage partners maintain separate residences for the purpose of work commitments in different geographic locations. The couple intends to remain married and they do not consider the separation as a precursor to divorce. The form is not new as ancient societies frequently had hunters and warriors absent from the family for long periods. Migrations, war, and prison all separate families and have for hundreds of years. In more recent times, wives and children might spend the summer months in a family home with only occasional visits from a working husband. What makes the commuter marriage unique, according to Govaerts "is that in this case the decision for a family separation considers the demands of the wife's career" (1985, p. 11). It also appears to be a well-educated middle class phenomenon (Gerstel & Gross, 1982).

The commuter lifestyle has drawbacks. Those who attempt it report experiencing feelings of loneliness and loss, particularly in the daily intimacy of their marriages that they had taken for granted. Many reported an unwelcome disruption in their sex life. For some, it was a result of being tired; others needed time to readjust when they did spend time together. Most reported feeling pressured to accomplish a great deal during their time together, and if expectations were not met, they felt keenly disappointed. Time was a factor and a number felt that one month was the outside limit for separations. Beyond that, spouses felt distanced from each other and reentry into an intimate relationship was difficult. Many felt that one or two week separations were ideal. Gerstel and Gross reported that couples who had a pattern of seeing each other every weekend were replicating a more familiar work leisure pattern adhered to by society. Those who saw each other at odd intervals reported their meetings as feeling awkward and strange.

An additional problem is that there is almost always additional work for the partner assigned the home and child care (Farris, in Rapoport & Rapoport, 1978). If there were children, the absent parent frequently reported feelings of guilt and dissatisfaction (Gross, 1980). Employers, family, and friends are not always supportive of the commuter marriage decision, especially if there are children. They often assume that the marriage is in trouble. The commuter couples reported that friends often excluded them from get-togethers, as they were no longer perceived as a couple. As for the reported extra marital affairs, those who had done so before continued to do so, and those who had not, did not begin. Furthermore, the lifestyle requires a great deal of added expense to maintain two residences, often duplicating household items. Additional transportation, telephone, and household services were frequently required.

With all the drawbacks, one wonders if there are compensations. Apparently, there are many. Gerstel and Gross (1982) report benefits of career mobility and development, with each person reporting that freedom from having to accommodate each others daily schedule enabled them to concentrate more fully on work if they chose to do so. Many reported heightened communication and a sense of rediscovery in the marital relationship, and a more equal distribution of household tasks, with husbands reporting they do more now, and wives less. Wives report that when living in the family home they felt more pressure "to keep a neat family home" (Gerstel & Gross, 1982 p. 84). Apparently, when freed from this responsibility, many women discovered that it was a self imposed pressure; a need to meet her own self image, one in relation to her husband, and appeared to be activated only when both spouses shared a single home. Living by themselves, women were able to think of themselves outside the role and are comfortable relaxing housekeeping standards.

> Commuter marriage and conventional marriage are - in this respect - mirror images. By living together, couples obtain intimacy but such intimacy may yield disenchantment or frustration. By living apart, couples rediscover each other at the cost of daily intimacies. Here, the costs and rewards of residential separation expose a basic, perhaps irreconcilable, dilemma of conventional marriage. (Gerstel & Gross, 1982, p. 83)

It appears that commuter marriage works best when; couples are motivated by, and find work central to their lives; they have adequate financial resources; are comfortable enough in their marriages; see each other regularly; and there are no children living in the home.

Quality of Life

Quality of life is still an issue and continues to be referred to in the 80s. For example, "In addition to these dual-career factors, we also are seeing the changing values of employees who expect a certain quality of life for the entire family" (Kahnweiler, 1988, p. 58).

Raymond and Eliot state "Employees and their spouses are revolting against the stress and insecurity of the mobile society. For them values have changed; quality of life is the key consideration" (1980, p. 62). Later in the article they say, "many corporations are providing consulting services to help employees cope with the stresses which often accompany a move" (ibid., p. 63). They believe that one of the keys to a successful transfer is to make sure that any employee who is being moved has the feeling of having made an informed personal choice rather than the feeling of being transferred arbitrarily by a decision from above.

Each generation also has its priorities and the quality of life issue remains a strong value. For some this might mean a large city; for others, a small town, good housing or an agreeable climate. Quality of life is subjective and each couple will have to evaluate what this means for them.

Studies on Children

Earlier research indicated that moving children at certain developmental stages could be disruptive for them. The first separation stage, occurring around preschool ages three to five, and the second separation stage, adolescence, from ages thirteen to sixteen were specifically mentioned. The belief was that preschoolers, in the process of separating from home and mother, are already adjusting their behavior patterns to a new authority figure. The changes involved in a relocation might strain their adaptive abilities. Adolescents are struggling to separate from dependent ties to their parents and rely heavily on their peers to successfully negotiate this stage. It is also an age of conformity. Removing them from the support of their peers, and placing them in what feels like an alien environment with different dress codes, hairstyles, and behaviors is greatly disturbing to them. "Except for the first two years of life, at no other time does a person experience as much physiological, anatomical, and cognitive change than during adolescence" (Erkut, 1986, p. 40). Simultaneously, during a relocation, teens are more dependent on their parents and feel pulled back into the family system from which they are struggling to separate.

Researchers and educators in the 80s continue to focus on these age groups building on the work of previous decades.

Jalongo addressed the needs of preschoolers when relocating and referred to Kaplan's work on infancy to describe how a young child acquires a sense of home. Kaplan believed that,

> The origins of our attachment to home are to be found in the infants earliest attachment to his (or her) mother, the mother he begins to use as a home base from which to explore the world . . . into ever widening circles of the unknown. From then on, though he may roam but a few feet, his body-mind is anchored by an image of home base. (in Jalongo, 1985, p. 51)

Jalongo believed that three-and-four-year-olds especially need stability and routine and to alter the concept of home when relocating can be traumatic for a young child.

Jones, a family therapist, agreed that young children are vulnerable, as they do not yet have the language skills to explain their feelings. In addition, they do not understand the concepts of distance and permanency and do not fully comprehend that they might not ever be able to see or play with their same little friends anymore. They can be devastated when they arrive at their destination and realize this. Jones reported on a study by Williams at UCLA that infants and children have more colds in the first few months after relocating and "an older child will express his or her grief and discomfort through behavior but an infant will express it somatically" (1984, p. 85).

Marsico and Puskar reported in Pediatric Nursing that children's coping mechanisms are usually underdeveloped and that "coping mechanisms such as fantasy, denial, withdrawal, anger, grieving and depression reflect the child's attempt to handle the move and the accompanying changes" (1986, p. 109). Both Marsico and Puskar, and Jones (1984) referred to the grief stages of denial, anger, bargaining, depression, and resolution following relocation. They stressed the importance of parents allowing children to work through the stages in their own time.

In an observational study of newcomers to a preschool class, Feldbaum, Christenson and O'Neal observed that the newcomers "exhibited signs of stress and ambivalence such as being immobile, muscularly tense, averting their gaze, rocking, shuffling, and playing with their clothing" (1980, p. 497). By week six, the newcomers were indistinguishable from the host group. They learned the behavior of the group from observation and pressure exerted from the host group to conform to the existing protocol, à la Bandura[7]. This was similar to an study by Phillips et al. (1951) mentioned earlier in this paper to illustrate how adaptive behaviors of mobile adults are learned in childhood. It would be reassuring for parents to know these behaviors are age appropriate in new situations and only if they continued for extended periods following relocations would intervention be deemed necessary.

In an article discussing research on children and relocation Smardo wrote that the responses of "loneliness, irritability and anger may be experienced by the child whose friend has moved away, just as they may be by the child who moves" (1981, p. 40). She also mentioned one of the few researchers, Inbar, who believed that the most vulnerable age was that of six to eleven years old. Inbar hypothesizes, according to Smardo, that moving during these years interferes with both language development and the socialization process.

In an effort to find out how schools helped newcomers meet new friends, educators Cornille, Bayer, and Smyth (1983) did a national survey of school systems. Because of the reported vulnerability of adolescent children, they focused on middle and junior high schools. The average length of time to make friends was reported to be 23 days, and for academic adjustment 17 days. According to the teachers the children who had the most difficulty adjusting

[7] Albert Bandura is considered to be an authority on social learning theory which attributes changes in behavior to observation and imitation.

to the new school were those who were large or small for their age, had physical handicaps, poor self concept, were older or younger than their classmates, or exceptional academically. For these children, a longer adjustment time was necessary. The schools also had mixed results with *newcomers clubs* and some felt that they could label the child an outsider and impede assimilation. Most children reported that lunchtime was the most difficult period and they feared eating alone. Schools reported the best success with one-on-one programs in which students volunteered as big sisters and brothers spending time with the new students, including lunchtime, to help them through the adjustment period. Counselors stressed the importance of scheduling a meeting with the new student during the second or third week as this was often a time when problems surfaced.

One of the biggest concerns for children in moving is their peer relationships. "The changing identity of the adolescent is anchored in his or her relationship to others. These relationships can confirm new roles as they develop and provide support in other areas" (Gullotta, Donohue, and Zinger, in Voles, 1982, p. 73). The majority of children stated "that leaving old friends was the main dislike of moving, while meeting new friends was the best part" (Smardo, 1981, p. 42).

Apparently, children in all age categories found that leaving their old friends was the most difficult part of moving. They found it even more difficult than entering a new school or making new friends. See Table 3 below.

Table 3. Parents' reports of children's problems associated with their most recent move

(Brett, 1982, p. 460)

Problem	Age at last move							
	1-5 Years		*6-14 Years*		*15-18 Years*		*Total*	
	Boys	**Girls**	**Boys**	**Girls**	**Boys**	**Girls**	**Boys**	**Girls**
Missing old friends	52%	49%	75%	81%	94%	85%	71%	72%
Missing relatives	33%	26%	17%	33%	33%	22%	24%	30%
Making new friends	18%	10%	24%	31%	67%	54%	26%	27%
Adjusting to school	10%	16%	32%	33%	33%	50%	27%	28%
Insecurity	24%	16%	25%	28%	17%	25%	24%	24%
Dependency	30%	17%	18%	29%	28%	8%	22%	23%
Finding work	–	–	–	–	42%	17%	–	–
Number of children	61	51	126	102	18	13	207	166

Note: Data based on parental reports. Parents were given the option to indicate that the problem was not relevant to their child.

A Fortune article by Kiechel (1987) quotes pediatric psychiatrist Donald Bechtold as saying that children of executive nomads are good at making friends quickly. It's the deeper long lasting friendships that they have difficulty with, and this pattern may continue to adulthood.

Brett (in Cooper & Payne, 1980) reported that while mobile teenagers had "less well-developed peer relationships than stable teenagers" (p. 129) there was no evidence to indicate that moving negatively impacted other areas of their life, e.g. their relationships with their parents, their mental health, or their school achievement.

Researchers have noted that parents tend to over-estimate their children's mental abilities and their capacity to adapt. When children self-report, the findings are frequently less positive. A study by Hutton, Roberts, Walker, and Zuniga (1987), conducted on ninth graders, used a modification by Chandler of the Coddington's Life Events Scale for Children[8] (in Hutton et al., 1987). The adults rated the events as they believed the children would rate them. What adults perceive to be stressful in a child's life appears to be different from what the child perceives to be stressful (see Table 4).

Table 4. Adult/Student stress rating
(Data from Hutton, Roberts, Walker & Zuniga, 1987)

Adults rated the following life events as more stressful than students who rated them	**Students rated the following life events as more stressful than adults who rated them**
Jail sentence of a parent	Change in child's acceptance by peers
Severe illness requiring hospitalization of parent	Family moves
Having a visible congenital deformity	Mother beginning work
Increase in the number of arguments between parents	Loss of job by parent
Becoming involved with drugs and alcohol	Poor grades in school
Marriage of parent to step-parent	Birth of brother or sister
Increase in number of arguments with parents	Increased arguments with brothers and sisters
Frequent absence of one or both parents	Vision problem requiring glasses
Illness requiring hospitalization of brother or sister.	

[8] Similar to the Homes Rahe Stress Test (1967) but developed specifically for children.

Perception appears to be a recurring theme in stress studies as well as social support. In a study of how adolescents cope with the stress of relocation, Donohue and Gullotta (1983) examined coping behaviors of high school students. The students were from upper middle class mobile corporate families and had moved anywhere from four to fourteen times. The instrument used was a modified version of the Spouses' Coping Inventory (McCubbin & Dahl, 1975).

According to Donohue and Gullotta the most important range of coping behaviors were those that established supportive relationships and friendships, and "the young women in this study found a number of coping behaviors significantly more helpful than their male counterparts" (1983, p. 400). They hypothesized that perhaps there were questions missing from the inventory that would have applied to the males, or that the males were modeling the coping behaviors of their corporate fathers who have been found to be "emotionally less expressive than males in other working environments" (ibid.).

Blotnick, a psychologist, and his staff monitored over 1,700 moves of clients over a ten-year period. They reported that over two thirds of the families had "considerable distress" (1985, p. 214), not all of which was evident at the time. Moves that involved children accounted for most of the serious difficulties, with teens having the most difficulty according to Blotnick. With over 900 teens in his sample, Blotnick found some patterns of behavior. He established that the teens either became more extroverted or more reclusive than they had been previously. They also tried to impress their classmates with material possessions or by giving parties. The most successful route to acceptance was being outstanding in a sport. These friendships developed more quickly and endured longer.

Blotnick said that he found that corporate children had a more difficult time than the children of the military did. He attributed this to the fact that military bases are built to look identical worldwide, but the cities that corporate families are sent to may be vastly different. He believed that more adaptive resources were required of the corporate children.

Adolescence and Self-Concept

Kroger found, in her study of the relationship between mobility and self-concept in adolescents, that it was not the number of moves but the distance that had an impact on adolescents. She reported a significant negative correlation between distance of moving and self-concept; the greater the distance moved, the lower the self-concept score. She believed that the finding supported the theories of Mead and Erikson who stressed the importance of environmental continuity for the development of a healthy self-concept. The greater the distance moved, the greater the likelihood of more drastic changes in environment. "One defines self according to how one sees others responding to it" (1980, p. 967). One then synthesizes and integrates this with earlier childhood identifications into a coherent whole. When one encounters inconsistency in feedback, it may result in greater difficulty in forming a consistent whole. This study is relevant to corporate families as corporate families make more long distance moves than the general population.

Sanders (1984) examined the relationship between mobility and self-concept in high school and junior high pupils. While he did not find significant relationships in his older group, he did find significant negative relationships between mobility and self-concept in middle school students. He concluded however, that the data indicated that the relationship might not be a causal one as he believed that race, socioeconomic status, and parental marital status confounded the factor of mobility. Hendershott (1989) agreed, and added that one should include the control variables of age, gender, family structure, intra-family relationships, academic achievement, and friendships when assessing the effects of mobility.

As families become more complex with blended family relationships and changing roles, it may become increasingly difficult to test for the effects of mobility on the family. It does help explain however, why some of the data appear contradictory.

Positive Studies

Stroh believed that the popular press sensationalized the negative effects of mobility on the family. In her study of the effects of mobility on corporate children she found, "no long-term negative effects associated with a mobile childhood characterized by multiple moves, as opposed to a relatively stable one in which one might expect perhaps a single move" (1989, p. 66). Neither did she find short-term effects. The children in her study "did not differ significantly from children who did not move on measures of social, behavioral, school, physical adjustment and self-confidence" (ibid.). She found the best predictor for future adjustment was prior adjustment and that mobile children whose parents were well adjusted, were themselves well adjusted. In addition, those children who were allowed input into the moving decision were better adjusted following the move. While the study design incorporated telephone interviews with the children, the majority of the data were based on parental reports. Stroh found the parental and children's reports significantly related. "Some researchers have noted that when responding to questionnaires, parents underestimate their children's problems or overestimate their ability" (Barrett & Noble; Miller; in Stroh, 1989, p. 29).

One observation on this particular study should be mentioned. The quality of the relationships was not measured. Parents may cite numbers of friends or groups their child is involved with as an indicator of adjustment. Previous researchers have observed that one may have many superficial relationships without finding them satisfying or feeling supported by them (Lin et al., 1981). Others have observed that mobile children are adept at presenting themselves as friendly and outgoing, enabling them to fit in more readily. In private, many corporate children say they feel like outsiders (Gullotta et al., 1981; Schetky, 1982; & Stroh, 1989).

Brett, who was Stroh's advisor on her study, conducted a study funded by the ERC[9], called "Job Transfer and Well Being." Both Stroh's study and Brett's study used the same sample group of 350 mobile corporate employees and their families. Brett observed that the sample was "probably biased in the direction of respondents with positive attitudes towards moving" (1982, p. 461). The study found that mobile employees and their wives were more satisfied with their lives, families, and marriages than were stable employees and their wives; however, mobile employees and their wives were less satisfied with social relationships. Moving was found to create problems for children, but there was little evidence that mobility is related to lasting social integration problems. Friedman (1989) observed that Brett's control group was not as similar as one would like, and the executives had not been recently transferred; the results may reflect continuous upheaval and not a single transfer event.

Erkut (1986), in an article on moving with teenagers, said that even though many adolescents react negatively to most moves, not all do. It depends on what else is going on in their life at the time. If there are too many other

[9] See footnote page 77.

stresses, then the move may be overwhelming. However, there are times when the move can be a solution if the adolescent has had problems in the present location. The move can give them a fresh start.

Cornille et al. in their survey of newcomer programs for adolescents said, "generally, children successfully deal with relocation after a brief period of stress and disorganization" (1983, p. 229) and added that moving helps some children develop new talents and skills.

Berry in her book on corporate couples, said that the couples reported the good and bad points of the lifestyle. The negatives were,

> no place to call home, no longtime close friends, a lack of closeness with their own families, and the loneliness of the rootless. Conversely, they listed the positives as, personal growth, seeing and experiencing new places and people, financial security and the sense of accomplishment and goal fulfillment. (1985, p. 61)

Marsico and Puskar in an article in Pediatric Nursing quoted the earlier 1972 study by Mann who found "that highly mobile college students possessed more flexibility, autonomy, independence and cognitive complexity" than students who were not mobile (Mann, in Marsico & Puskar, 1986, p. 108). Goebel said, "mobility had a positive effect on cognitive development and better prepared children for adult independence" (Goebel, in Marsico & Puskar, 1986, p. 108).

Oglesby studied relocation stress in adult corporate movers and non-movers. Only 4% said the relocation was not stressful; 35% found it slightly stressful; 46% moderately stressful; and 15% very stressful. Despite the relatively high stress ratings, the movers considered themselves "successful compared with others, pleased with themselves in general, emotionally strong, and generally in good health for their ages" (1985, p. 132). This would be consistent with Gullotta and Donohue's (1981b) observations that despite the hardships that frequent relocation imposed, corporate families were committed to the lifestyle.

Pinder (1989) wrote of his observations based on three different studies involving more than 800 managers and spouses spanning over a decade. While he enumerated the negatives, namely difficulties with older children's high school adjustment, difficulty developing close friendships, and the inability to put down roots, he also said that the transferees listed many benefits of moving. Some of these were seeing new places, meeting new people, career advancement, and financial gain. Pinder thought that it was ironic that highly mobile people enjoyed meeting new people, but were not able to stay in places long enough to develop close friendships, which only can be accomplished over time.

Veiga (1981), in his study of two thousand managers, said that the mobile managers believed that their careers had benefited from mobility. He believed that many had bought into the *unlimited success theory* and that they enjoyed being mobile. The manager believed that being mobile gave them broad business exposure as well as career opportunities, both of which enhanced their reputation so that others respected their opinions and sought their advice.

Discussion

Those who defend corporate relocation insist that the impact of relocation is vastly overrated, and that most transfers benefit the corporations, employees, and their families. It appears from the research that relocation may assist in the attainment of career and financial goals.

Consistent with the earlier decades, some families appear to move well. However, it appears that a relocation is most often experienced by the family as a stressful situation, with potential short-term distress and long-term implications.

The short-term distress seems to arise from the fact that each family member may perceive the relocation differently, and progress through the stages at a different rate. Communication may break down at a time when it is crucial to have good communication, because the family system is undergoing many changes.

In addition, if after repeated relocations the family becomes a tightly closed system, they may not accept outside help when offered or seek outside help when needed. This has implications for the increasing numbers of complex dual-career and non-traditional families who are most in need of support when relocating. It may put them more at risk during relocation than traditional families.

The long-term implications involve the entire family system. Members of a closed nuclear family may have difficulty forming close intimate friendships with outsiders. This may not only leave family members feeling that something is lacking in their life, but may strain the family system as it attempts to meet all of the intimacy and friendship needs of its members. This may also make the launching stage of young adults more difficult for the family.

Therapists working with mobile corporate families have commented on their commitment to the lifestyle and their resistance to change. This indicates that the families may be willing to accept the drawbacks of a mobile lifestyle in order to reap the benefits of career and financial gain.

In addition to stress: depression, isolation, grief, and a sense of loss continue to be themes in the 80s. The results are consistent with previous decades, and socialization may partly explain why men and women experience relocation differently.

Studies on children continue, and there is concern that families move frequently during the childrearing stages of the life cycle. Repeated relocations continue to be mentioned as especially difficult for children during adolescence and the early preschool years. It appears that children are at risk in developing poor peer relationships, but that mobility does not necessarily affect their mental health or academic studies.

The complexity of mobility as a factor continues to evolve. Earlier researchers found that socioeconomic and educational level as well as I.Q. should be accounted for in mobility studies. By the 80s perception, culture, age, gender, personality, intra-family structure, and coping skills are all added as variables that may affect how the family experiences a relocation. The study of mobility appears to be as complex as the families themselves.

The change in values that appeared to have taken place in the previous decade has continued as well. Work is no longer seen as a total source of identity. Today's corporate employees appear to value their personal life, and the family continues to be looked to for comfort and satisfaction.

More changes will take place in the 90s as these *baby-boomers* move into upper management. These are the families that have experienced first hand the difficulties in attempting to maintain a dual-career lifestyle. They will be more open to flextime, job sharing and telecommuting. Just as they pioneered the dual-career and commuter lifestyle, in the 90s these families will pioneer new ways to work.

CHAPTER VIII

1990-95: TECHNOLOGY COMES HOME

The real question is not whether machines think, but whether men do [1]

The story of movement and change, present in every decade, emerged in the 90s in the field of technology. The ostentation of the 80s had vanished and the recession tightened its grip all across America. Companies were *downsizing* and *restructuring* in order to keep pace with rapidly changing technology. The automated workplace created unemployment for some, and others needed retraining in necessary skills. Flexibility and adaptability became key words for business survival.

Technology also altered the ways that families and corporations interacted. At the start of the decade, it was estimated that 92% of American households were connected to cable television. People began ordering goods via television, and *surfing the net* became popular for the increasing number of homes with computers. Families started using electronic mail (e-mail) to communicate and stay connected the way long letters and calls home had done in the past. As the computer connected home and the office, working from home became not only possible but also a reality for millions.

The changing workplace was becoming *family friendly*

[1] B. F. Skinner in Kosko, 1993, p. 268.

and *politically correct*. *Sexual harassment* was making headline news in business, the military, and the highest levels of government.

A country already in recession became even more subdued as American troops went as peacekeepers to Bosnia and then prepared for a war in the Gulf. For the first time in history, the world watched a war begin on television. Broadcast live, it held millions spellbound around the world. Technology had also produced *smart* weapons of mass destruction, awesome in their power, but ultimately shortening the war. Worldwide, civil wars broke out in Bosnia and Rwanda, and Haitians took to boats to escape carnage at home.

Americans also faced bloodshed at home. The World Trade Center in New York was bombed, killing six and injuring more than 1,000. This was followed by the single worst instance of domestic terrorism in U.S. history, the bombing of the Alfred P. Murrah Federal Building in Oklahoma City. The final death toll of 169 included 19 children. American confidence was shaken, and the mood remained somber. It would take until the middle of the decade for the economy to rebound, but when it did, the morale of the American people was restored and unemployment dropped to its lowest point in decades.

The quality of life issue remained strong and corporations offered more support services and incentives to relocating families, finally acknowledging the systems interaction between work and family. Mobility rates continued their slow decline nationwide. The 16.7% for 1993-94 was down from the 20% annual mobility rates of the previous decades.

Fewer Americans were moving but two of the main reasons they had always moved remained the same. They were moving for work and for opportunity. Many still viewed relocation as the *fast track* to corporate success and women began to realize that relocation might be a way to break through the *glass ceiling*. By 1993, women comprised 16% of transferees, and the number continued to rise.

Dual-career families continued to increase and, in a 1993 article, Hanks and Sussman estimated that nearly 75% of transfers involved dual-career families. By the year 2000 it was estimated that the percentage of dual-career families would increase to 85% (Roman, 1992). As the sandwich generation, these families were requesting more assistance for childcare and in moving elderly parents.

However, for these relocating families of the 90s many of the familiar problems surrounding relocation remained, only now they were magnified by the complexity of their family systems.

Grief and the Stages of Relocation in the 90s

By the 90s the grief stages had become accepted as a part of the relocation process for the trailing spouse and children (Hendershott, 1995).

Similar to the previous generations of authors, Loomis, in her study on spouse reaction to relocation said, “some authors have specifically likened the transition experience to the process of grieving a death” (1992, p. 14). She reported that the participants in her study experienced anger, sadness, and frustration and that while some responses were positive, the “emotional consequences of relocation were overwhelmingly negative” (ibid., p. 87).

Loth (1990) in her article on relocation for Mobility magazine, also referred to the stages. She said that psychologists refer to the five stages as shock, denial, anger, depression, and acceptance. When one undergoes a change such as a relocation, one will experience these emotions.

A workbook approach by Porter and Rand (1992) for families on the move offered practical help, but also used the stages to explain the psychological process of relocation. They said it was not unusual to take as long as two years to feel at home in a new location and that if one could not seem to make it through a stage, then counseling was advisable. Solomon (1993) also cited the two-year adjustment time and suggested with corporate moves that the employees ask for a mentor in the new location.

Olkowski and Parker, in their book guiding parents on ways to help their children deal with moving said, “a child's reaction to the realities of moving are similar to those of patients confronting a terminal illness” (1993, p. 22). They then summarized the five stages and also listed verbal and behavioral cues to help parents recognize stress reactions in their children. For example; children becoming quiet and withdrawn, angry or fearful, or experiencing sleeplessness or nightmares. They stressed to parents the importance of the family openly discussing their feelings about the move, and validating those feelings.

Schoeni, writing for EAP Digest described the stages and referred to them as a "cluster of feelings triggered by a move" (1991, p. 34). She stressed that not only did the length of the stages differ for each family member, but the effects as well.

McCollum (1990) examined the stages in detail in her text on relocation. She said the reason that the grief stage is so intense is that it triggers past grief, whether one is aware of it or not. This causes one to relive past separations and losses, which may be extremely painful.

Hendershott discussed the stages in her book, but said that while the pattern may still apply to some, many spouses do not see themselves as victims in the moving process. She said that myths about corporate wives tend to divide them into two categories. There is the ideal, cheerful, and supportive dream wife and the problem baggage wife. Hendershott says that she is not sure that the "ideal" (1995, p. 39) corporate wife ever existed, and that it is certainly not true of dual-career families today.

The reality may be that corporate wives presented the ideal picture to the corporations because they believed it was in the best interest of their husbands' career to do so. The category of spouse that "spousal mobility syndrome" (ibid., p. 42) might refer to, according to Hendershott, is the homemaker trailing spouse, because she experiences a loss of identity. The "homemaker spouses who have not worked outside the home suffer because they are moving from being 'someone' in their neighborhood or community, to being someone's wife, or mother only" (ibid., p. 43).

While this sounds surprisingly similar to Seidenberg's (1973) description of corporate wives in the 70s, Hendershott explained that there are really three generations of corporate wives. Wives 45 and older do not typically work outside the home if their husband is a top-level executive. They did not question transfers and saw their duty as being a supportive partner in their husbands career. The second generation of wives, 35 to 45, are the ones caught in the middle. They received the message from society that it was all right to have their own career. However, it was clear that the expectations of the senior corporate executives and their spouses at the company were that they should replicate the first generation. These women feel torn and experience the most stress. It is the third generation, men and women in their twenties or early thirties, who with rare exception, all expect to have careers and are comfortable with their decision to do so. The women in this age group may put careers on hold to have a family, but prefer to maintain independence from the corporation. The first generation of women are more likely to see relocation in terms of emotional loss; the second and third generation, in terms of career loss.

Familiar Themes

By now loss, depression, anomia, gemeinschaft, and attachment to place have become familiar themes and continue to be mentioned in the 90s as well.

According to McCollum (1990), whether the move was voluntary or not, all of the women she questioned experienced feelings of loss. Loomis (1992) however, quoted Brett (1982) as saying that when one could not influence the relocation decision, then one was more vulnerable to the negative effects of the move.

It may be that the more intense feelings are experienced by those with the least amount of control. Perhaps that is why some children experience such strong feelings following a relocation, as they generally have the least control of all over the moving decision

One of the most important losses according to McCollum (1990) was the loss of valuable support networks. McCollum explained the 1971 views of Jacobson, which she said were similar to those expressed by Freud in 1917. That is, that grief was a state of sadness; an emotional response caused by loss, in particular, a loss of some form of pleasure.

In contrast to grief, depression involved an aggression conflict, either in reality or within the psyche. When one is unable to resolve the conflict, the anger may turn inward. At the core of the depression, McCollum says, is the failure to resolve the conflict. This results in a loss of self-esteem. Grief then, according to McCollum, "is a state of sadness provoked by loss; depression is a state of diminished self-esteem provoked by failure" (1990, p. 65).

While clinicians think of depression as pathological, Jacobson and Zetzel (in McCollum, 1990), both say that it may be an appropriate or normal response when faced with disappointments in life.

Another familiar problem emerged as McCollum (1990) quoted Brett (1982) saying that the participants in her study were less satisfied with all aspects of their social relationships. McCollum referred to this gemeinschaft (1990, p. 246) as a feeling of togetherness or community, and said that just as those in Brett's study felt this to be lacking in their lives, the women in her study felt this lacking in their lives as well. McCollum said that her women reported feeling lonely, isolated, and at times, invisible in the community.

Toliver also mentions relocating families as being attracted to a community with gemeinschaft qualities. She described this as one where the residents would have "shared experiences and outlooks, and one in which primary relationships could develop" (1993, p. 124).

The single women in McCollum's 1990 study saw the move as an opportunity for growth and change. For those with partners, there was the feeling expressed by some of the women that while they had shared in the moving decision, the move was expected of them. They had never seriously considered not moving with their men. This group was conforming to society's expectations, without the awareness that this was, in part, controlling their decision.

Pfau (1990) mentions another recurring theme, a sense of place, in a study on transferring students. Pfau quotes work by Newman and Newman in which they address the issue of how children adapt to school change and recreate the "sense of neighborhood" (Newman & Newman, 1978, in Pfau, 1990, p. 22). Newman and Newman believed that the strong emotional attachments of friends, buildings, and spaces were crucial in understanding the losses experienced by children. They believed that the amount of stress experienced by children to be dependent on age, gender, and whether or not they perceived the relocation to be an opportunity for them. Newman and Newman found that it took several months for children to adapt under the best of circumstances. In addition, they believed that children who had moved before could carry that sense of place from the previous neighborhood. This formed a schema, which they applied to the new setting, and it facilitated their adaptation.

Settles also refers to a sense of place as the structure that helps the family develop its patterns. She said that "when returning to the neighborhood of one's youth, a search for familiar buildings and natural scenes is often the first activity undertaken in order to establish this sense of identity through the stability of environment" (1993, p. 7).

In addition, if the buildings or scenes are no longer the same, the person experiences a sense of loss and the visit may be a disappointment for them.

McCollum describes this in terms of relocation and says that this sense of connection extends beyond the dwelling, into the physical surroundings. For those who have moved, "nostalgia for place can be intense" (1990, p. 71).

Many Americans appear to cherish memories of a childhood home and place great significance on birthplaces. A recent New York Times article about Presidential birthplaces said that millions of Americans make pilgrimages to the birthplaces of famous people, especially Presidents. The article said that in visiting the birthplace there was a feeling of experiencing the essence of a person. A Presidential birthplace with humble beginnings, such as President Clinton's near the railroad tracks, the article said, speaks to who we are as a people for it places us in a democracy.

Place and *Community* are important because the organization of the family is strongly influenced by the community systems it interacts with. The community will serve to either reinforce the family's perspective or *worldview* by sharing similar beliefs, or bring stress to the family system if the family perceives that it is in a hostile environment. A family's beliefs shape how they view a stressful situation as well, according to Mettelman (1993).

Beliefs, she says, are formed through our culture and personal experience. They may be specific beliefs in a Supreme Being or a belief that one is in control of their life or not. Beliefs, therefore, affect how the family views the stressful situation and affects how the family copes with that stress.

Stress and the Family System in the 90s

Writers in the 90s frequently discuss the family as a system of interdependent people whose interactions influence each other and affect wider systems as well (Lundy, 1994).

Hendershott said,

> Few, if any, situations represent the convergence of as many conflicting demands and needs from as many areas as a move for work. All of the needs, real or perceived, held by the corporation, the employee, the spouse, the children, the community and the economy overlap. (1995, p. 8)

Cornille and Brotherton (1993) discuss how stress and the absence of support can lead to problems in the family system during relocation. Cornille (1993), in a different article, discusses stress and relocation. Cornille refers to Holmes and Rahe (1967) and McCubbin et al. (1980b), and points out that a move is often coupled with other changes and this can lead to a pile-up of stress for the family system.

Pfau (1990) also mentions the cumulative stresses and discusses how families are interconnected emotionally during times of transition. Olkowski and Parker (1993), in their book on moving with children, refer to change as bringing with it the potential for stress as well as the potential for new experience.

McCollum (1990) mentions how moving destroys lines of communication and Robbins (1992) agrees. Robbins discusses jumbled family roles and the need for the family to reorganize following a relocation. Sussman and Settles (1993) discuss not only the family system but also the movement of peoples and how that movement affects people worldwide. Sussman and Settles (1993) take the position that what happens in one society affects all societies that come in contact with that society; Systems in it's broadest sense.

The Myth of Separate Worlds

One who does not agree that moving is stressful is Young, a psychologist working with relocating families. Young believes that relocation stress is a "myth" (1990a, p. 27) and while it has the potential to be stressful, it is not a certainty and depends on one's reaction to the event. He said that he disagreed with the use of the Holmes Rahe scale for relocation as "there was no data to back up the conclusion" (ibid., p. 28). In another article Young referred to the myth of separate worlds when he said there "always has been a tendency on the part of corporations to stay out of the personal lives of their employees" (1990b, p. 66). In discussing the corporate work force, Young said that there would be more of a need for involvement and assistance to the relocating families of the future. This was because of all of the demands and needs of dual-career families such as care of children and aging parents, spouse job assistance, and help in running a household, that arise when both spouses have fulltime careers.

Stroh (1993) said that the relationship between work and family was complex and that we are just beginning to understand the ways that our work affects our personal lives.

In another relocation article, Bruzzese quotes a relocation executive who says, "many companies don't want to know about the personal side of relocation" (1994, p. 51).

Hanks and Sussman refer to the myth and say, "relocation has been part of the larger value system of which the long arm of the job has reached into family life" (1993, p. 100). Hanks and Sussman refer to the family and work systems and say that the linkages are reciprocal, that a shift took place in the mid 80s. Previously, families had subordinated their demands to work demands. The corporation had given little attention to the family, but as loyalty shifted from the corporation to the self, corporations began focusing on family concerns.

Jordan questioned this concern in an article on family issues and relocation wherein he said, "a generation ago, few large corporations would have discussed family issues related to relocation. . .today, corporations realize that ignoring family issues will affect the bottom line" (1995, p. 59). Moreover, Loomis (1992) said that few employers acknowledged the personal needs of relocating partners.

Schoeni (1991) spoke of the effects of relocation on not only the family but also the community, and said that company management must acknowledge the disruption and accept a portion of the responsibility.

Todd added that corporations have tried to cling to the notion that they bore no responsibility for their relocating families' concerns. However, with the increasing number of dual-career families, it was "no longer possible for them to deny the link between the two spheres of work and family" (1994, p. 2).

Dual-Career and Relocation

The career couple became the big challenge for relocation in the 90s. An article in Personnel Journal addressed this issue and said that the problem was complex. Not only were fewer couples willing to relocate when both had careers but, as the world became increasingly global, few companies had a well-organized program for dealing with the issues involved. "Even worse, most of these organizations believed that this problem was the couple's responsibility to resolve" (Reynolds & Bennett, 1995, p. 4). In many countries, spouses are not able to obtain work permits. "The loss of a second income and self esteem on the part of the trailing spouse, who often isn't able to find work, can cause serious problems and put the couple at a higher risk for divorce" (ibid.). The article also stated that even in traditional families that are sent on overseas assignments, the divorce rate is higher than average. Capell discussed a recent survey of almost 2,000 relocated career couples conducted by the University of Tennessee in 1994.

The dual-career families had the most stress, according to Capell (Figure 10).

Figure 10. - Survey of relocated corporate employees (Capell, 1996, p. R6)

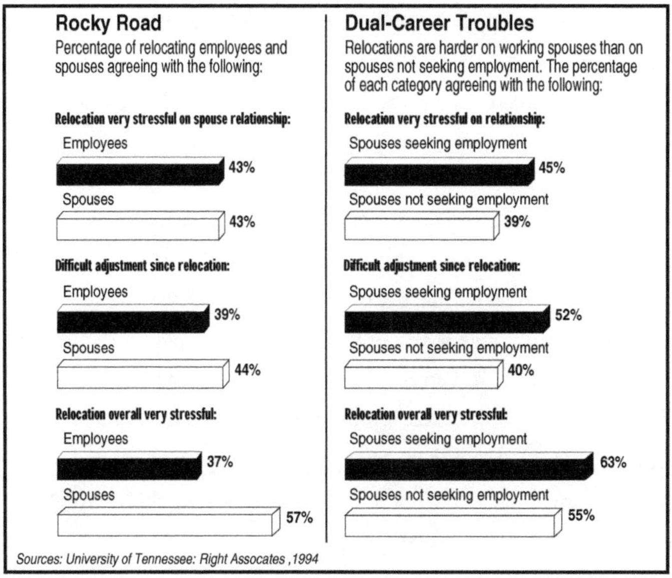

Capell said, "37% said that their transfer had been very stressful, while 20% said that, at some point since their move, they had considered quitting their current jobs" (1996, p. R6). Some corporations have started innovative programs to assist relocating families in the 90s. This includes more flexible coverage of travel, housing, and visitation for commuter couples, the relaxing of anti-nepotism policies, and the development of job banks for accompanying spouses.

Porter and Rand addressed the dual-career issue and said that one of the biggest challenges that dual-career couples face is the question of whose career has priority; and that "even the best and most equitable relationships can be seriously challenged by a move" (1992, p. 18).

Reynolds and Bennett also addressed the dual-career issue and mentioned its recent growth. "By 1995, the U.S. Dept. of Labor predicts that 81% of all marriages will be dual-career partnerships" (1991, p. 46). They said that some employers still take the position that the private lives of their employees are their own affair and should not be a subject of consideration by the company. The authors added that sometimes, assistance for relocating couples by the corporation was so limited, they were expected to make crucial decisions without adequate information. This included data on labor market conditions and what basic supports such as daycare and maintenance services were available in the new location.

The Trailing Spouse

When the term *trailing spouse* was originally used for a relocating couple, the employee with the job offer was usually male and the spouse female. Some found the term demeaning, and thought it brought to mind a "caveman moving onto a sunny slope dragging his woman by the hair, kicking and screaming, with the kids 'trailing' behind" (Kelley, 1995, p. 93). Kelley suggested the term "relocating partner" (ibid.) which appears to be a more appropriate term for the couples of the 90s.

In 1987, 12% of relocating partners were male, and the estimates were that number would increase to 19% by the year 2000 (Cetron et al., 1987). Cetron's predictions appeared to be on track, for "by 1993, women comprised 16% of the transferee base; today they account for a quarter of all transferees" (*Runzheimer Reports on Relocation,* in Moving on up, Newsbreak, 1996). In another article, Cetron said that in some companies the proportion was even higher. "State Farm Insurance, for example, reports that 60% of its trailing spouses are men" (1993, p. 74). Cetron et al. said, "Trailing husbands currently have different needs than the typical trailing wife, but time will blur some of those differences" (1987, p. 41). Those differences involved career development assistance for the husbands as opposed to simply job assistance, but Cetron et al. predicted that wives would need this more in the future. Another major difference according to Cetron et al. is in the level of support accorded the male relocating partner. While females are given sympathy and support, males are often objects of curiosity, even scorn. According to Crosby and Nightingale, when women began entering professional careers, they had to battle for years to get employers to realize they were as serious as their male counterparts. Now, said the authors, married men who relocate for the sake of their wives are going to have to fight that same battle. Crosby and Nightingale said that the men hear comments such as "Takes a lot of guts," or, "So, you're going to let her be the breadwinner" (1986, p. 36).

For this growing segment of the population, just as with the commuter marriages, these families may feel particularly isolated. They receive limited familial and societal support, and have few role models to follow. They may be particularly vulnerable following relocation.

The Changing Family System

The "Leave it to Beaver era" (Fusco, 1990, p. 80), a profile of the white male with two kids and a wife at home, is dead, according to an executive with a relocation firm in New York. Today, diversity is the rule, not the exception, and less than one child in three lives in a 1950's style nuclear family. "Of new hires in the 1990s, fully 92% will be women, an ethnic minority, foreign-born, or handicapped. In the year 2000, only about 31% of first-time job-seekers will not fit into these categories" (Cetron, 1993, p. 74).

While it may seem that this new family structure is a radical change from the past, Settles points out that the literature of small town America often reflects a picture of non-traditional families as part of American life. A closer look at Twain's (1875) novels reveal Huck Finn as an abandoned or foster child, and Tom Sawyer as a child reared in an extended family (Settles, 1993).

In addition, as a nation of immigrants, America has always been engaged in the process of assimilating newcomers into the culture. What the figures mean for relocation, though, is a different matter. Traditional lifestyles of the past allowed whole families to be relocated for one spouse's career. The accompanying partner provided the support, arranged the move, and attended to the needs of the family. With today's changing families, relocation needs are changing too. There are currently 68 million American adults, 36% of the adult population, who are classified as single (Conklin, 1991). Single-parent families are common, headed by both men and women. For this sandwich generation there may be custody arrangements to be considered, as well as extra time needed by singles during a move to arrange for special needs of children or parents (Fusco, 1990). Dual-career couples may be focused on finding a job for the relocating partner and these families may also be comprised of *partners*; the approximately 2.6 million unmarried couples living together in the U.S. (Cetron, 1993). In addition, according to Cetron, there are currently more than 800,000 couples of homosexual males, and about 750,000 lesbian pairs. Between the two groups, they are raising 92,000 children. These changing families may have concerns and needs that must be addressed in order for the move to go smoothly. Corporations must be sensitive to these families and have flexible policies in order to meet their needs.

Alternative Work Styles

As America was growing more aware of alternative lifestyles, corporations were becoming more aware of alternative work styles. Flextime provided employees with variations in the standard 9-5 workday. Job sharing enabled two individuals to be responsible for one job; and, home commuting enabled workers to complete assigned tasks at home. This telecommuting also enabled disabled and older workers to compete in the job market and eliminated transportation costs to work. These more flexible schedules enabled families, including dual-career and singles, to work out parenting schedules The goal being a more family friendly workplace (Zunker, 1990).

Commuter Marriage

The commuter marriage lifestyle that began in the 80s, as a way to deal with dual-careers and relocation, continued to be studied in the 90s. It had previously been observed that while commuting could be an equalizing force in the division of domestic chores, early socialization affected the way the couples themselves, as well as society, viewed the arrangement. Gerstel and Gross (1982) had found that commuter couples were using traditional couples to judge their relationship. It had also been suggested that if the couples used traditional role models then society would too. A study of commuter dual-career couples in the 90s revealed that the dual-career wives still had more household tasks than their husbands did, and the tasks still tended to be gender linked.

> All of the major tasks ascribed to the males are ones that must be attended to only periodically, examples such as lawn mowing, payment of bills, and washing cars. In contrast, most of the tasks ascribed to the female are either daily or weekly responsibilities, examples are preparing meals, daily care of children and pets, picking up clutter, and doing laundry or vacuuming. (Anderson & Spruill, 1993, p. 143)

Anderson and Spruill said that they found their results surprising as they had expected to find the commuter dual–career couples less tradition bound than other couples. Of the 39 couples in their study 74% said they and their spouse were pleased with their decision to commute. Many of the couples reported little role strain, suggesting that they were coping well with their decision. Despite the fact that these couples were considered highly educated and sophisticated by the researchers, they had not used a very systematic decision making process; nor had they considered all the alternatives or collected all the necessary information before making such a major life-style decision. Anderson and

Spruill (1993) suggested that since dual-career commuter marriages are likely to increase in the future, couples use counseling, understand and discuss all of the alternatives, and learn coping strategies before embarking on such a major decision.

Hendershott (1995) also discussed the commuter marriage in her book on relocation in the 90s. She referred to the work of Gerstel and Gross in the 80s and described the common pattern of establishing two households with the main reason being the dual-career concern, not uprooting children. Hendershott says that it is difficult to estimate how many commuter marriages there are today because the census bureau assumes co-residency for couples. "But, researchers estimated that there are over one million commuter marriages in the United States" (1995, p. 80). Moreover, Hendershott says, the number is growing. This is also due to the recognition on the part of this generation that each person has the right to seek self-actualizating pursuits. This was a right always assumed for males. What is new is the application of these rights to women. Hendershott says that even today, "neither human resource personnel from the corporations, nor relocation counselors or managers from the corporate relocation companies, ever suggest that there may be alternatives to family relocation" (ibid.). There is still pressure placed on the employee to encourage the spouse to relocate, otherwise the employee is viewed as less committed to the corporation. Some companies actually put policies in place to discourage commuter marriages. Others take the attitude that the corporation simply offers the relocation to the employee and it is up to the family to make it succeed.

Hendershott says that there is "corporate bias against commuter marriage" (ibid., p. 83) which she believes is rooted in the fact that commuter marriages violate the cultural norms about married couples living together.

In discussing the relocation history of these couples, Hendershott said that over 90% had made earlier relocation decisions based on the husband's career. As the couples realized the inequity of the situation, the decision was reached to attempt a commuter marriage. This was a way of demonstrating both spouses' commitment not only to their own career but their spouse's career.

It appears, even into the 90s, the commuter marriage is viewed with skepticism by family and friends who have great difficulty accepting the lifestyle and continue to exert pressure on the couple to conform to more traditional norms. The couples find it difficult to make friends and find support for their decision.

From a systems perspective the family boundaries become blurred, as the family members do not know how to view the couple. It is difficult for them to be perceived as a couple, yet they are neither divorced, nor single. They may be perceived to be in a fluid state by family members, and it may be that ambiguity that the family and friends find difficult and uncomfortable.

In addition, if corporations view those couples as less committed their long-range goal of career advancement may be defeated.

Systems and Roles

Family cohesion and functioning, according to Lundy, depend upon a value system that balances individual growth and autonomy with family unity. She says that corporate moves cause problems "when disparities in values among family members are exacerbated, imbalancing the adaptation process, and often, requiring more from some members than others" (1994, p. 102). One of the reasons for the shock of relocation has to do with the roles that women play in society, says Lundy. Historically, women accepted responsibility for the care and well-being of the family. Now that women are working full-time, society still assigns them that role and this creates role overload. This is evident particularly during a relocation. Women continue to feel responsible, not only for setting up the household, but for responding to the family's needs for nurturance. Parenting and caring for elderly relatives contribute significantly to role overload (McBride, 1990).

Settles said that men have also been placed in rigid roles, the main one being the "good provider" role (1993, p. 13). Men may resent their roles as well, according to Settles, for it places extreme pressure upon them to provide financially for the family. At the same time that women were taking on more roles, men's roles prescribed that they had little or no responsibility for the rest of the work of caring for the family.

Lundy believes that women are responding to society's messages that women are responsible for the care of the home and have been reluctant to turn over household tasks to their partners, who are also following prescribed roles. That is because "Gender roles are very slow to change" (1994, p. 110).

Earlier writers Stouffer and Lazarsfeld observed that "it is an old sociological hypothesis that the deeper the structure of an institution is rooted in the mores, the more resistant it is to change" (1972, p. 7). Lundy believes that when these necessary changes do not occur, both partners lose and, the family suffers. She said that there is a need to focus on all of the family systems, including the family of origin, in order to understand the systems interaction. Lundy believes that even though women feel that they are responsible for the emotional well-being of the family, "no one person can either cause or solve the family adjustment problems that may accompany a move" (1994, p. 107).

Children and Relocation in the 90s

According to the U.S. Bureau of Census, 10.8 million children under the age of eighteen move each year (Jensen, Copans & McCollum, 1995, p. 31). Children are generally the most involuntary movers of all, according to Jensen et al., and move only for one reason, because their parents have decided to relocate. "Many parents are unprepared for and overwhelmed by the impact moving has had on their children" (ibid.). The authors stress the importance of listening; that parents really listen to their children's concerns, and that professionals really listen to the family's concerns, so that these feelings and concerns will be validated.

Porter and Rand address children's reactions to relocation and say that for very young children, who do not have the ability to understand what is happening, it can be very confusing. For example, they do not know how to interpret having strangers walk through their house, and giving away or selling things. "If you give away a cat, can you give away a kid? When you sell the sofa does it mean that we will sit on the floor in our new house?" (1992, p. 10). While Porter and Rand believe that moving can be difficult for children of all ages they feel that "it is more painful for teens to move than their younger counterparts" (ibid., p. 13). Their peer ties must be broken, and their growth towards independence is not only put on hold, it is put into reverse. Porter and Rand are among several writers who suggest the possibility of boarding a teen with relatives or friends in order to finish high school.

Hendershott (1995) also believes that moving with children can be difficult and complex, but says that one should not generalize and assume that all children will react negatively to all moves. She believes that the most difficult time is junior high, which is due to the enormous changes in the development of the self during adolescence. As they begin to move from the family system at this age, they begin to develop their self-image from their peers. If their friends tell them they are funny or smart they internalize this and believe it to be true. The move takes them from an environment where they now know what it takes to be funny or smart and places them in an alien environment. They are fragile, and they do not know what it takes to be funny or smart in this strange territory.

Dickson (1995a) agreed that adolescence was a most difficult time and it was essential to involve children in the move from the very beginning. If possible, including them on pre-move visits to the new area.

In 1990, Brett, Stroh, and Reilly published a ten-year follow-up study by the ERC entitled the "Impact of Societal Shifts and Corporate Changes on Employee Relocation." The previous study by Herman and Werbel (1978) "The Effect of Job Transfer on Employees and Their Families" concluded that mobile employees and their families were dealing well with their mobile lifestyle. The 1990 study results relating to children were not quite as positive. This study concluded, "those teens who had moved more often, had a rougher time adjusting to their most recent move. As the number of moves increased, adjustment levels decreased" (p. 17). The most mobile teens were angrier about moving, liked their new school and classmates less, and had greater difficulty leaving grandparents and extended family. In addition, they fought more with their parents. This group of teens felt that they had less control over the moving decision. Their parents also perceived them to be "less well adjusted socially" (ibid.) than the parents of teens in the earlier study.

Stroh discussed the study in a later article and said, "despite the primary influence of the mother in the household, it was the father's well-being, not the mother's, that best predicted the teen's adjustment. The more well adjusted the father, the more well adjusted the teen" (1993, p. 47). Researchers in previous decades had tied children's well-being to the mother. From a systems perspective, if either parent is having trouble with the move, it is likely to impact the whole family. Stroh also observed that teenage girls were moved less frequently than teenage boys , but adjusted better long-term. However, they appeared to suffer more during the adjustment stages than their male counterparts.

Pfau, in her 1990 study on transferring students, referred to the higher number of transfers among low-income families. She said that there was an average of 20% to 30% of new school transfers annually in the public schools, but it was as high as 50% in schools serving low-income families.

Simpson and Fowler in 1994 published analysis of data from the 1988 National Health Interview Survey of Child

Health (NHIS) involving 10,362 school-age children and their families. They concluded that, "children who move three or more times are at increased risk for emotional/behavioral and school problems" (1994, p. 303). They also said that they believed that other characteristics of families, especially single parent or low income families, are related to mobility and children's emotional well-being. In another study, Long (1990) reported that children who were frequent movers often lived with a single parent and were economically disadvantaged. Simpson and Fowler said, "frequent moving may itself be a marker of greater family problems which lead to emotional stress in children" (1994, p. 308).

Wood, Halfon, Scarlata, Newacheck, and Nessim, using the same 1988 NHIS data, also did a study that was published in the Journal of the American Medical Association. They reached similar conclusions. "Frequent family relocation was associated with an increased risk of children failing a grade in school and four or more frequently occurring behavioral problems" (1993, p. 1334). Wood et al. said that relocation was frequently glorified in the United States as a characteristic of success and upward mobility. They said relocation also had a shadow side, which was that poor and minority families often move frequently because of economic deprivation, parental job loss, eviction, divorce, and/or death of a parent. "Families that are poor move 50% to 100% more frequently than families that are not poor" (ibid.). If the family is facing many concurrent stressors, this may overwhelm the family's coping mechanisms and compromise their ability to help the child adjust to the move. The information appeared to agree with what many other researchers had previously concluded, that moving could be harmful for children, particularly multiple moves. While these studies have serious implications for the general population, it is not necessarily true for all segments of the population. Researchers have previously pointed out (Whalen & Fried, 1973; Long, 1975; Lacey & Blane, 1979) that many studies on mobility do not apply to a well-educated middle class population. Corporate families may be dealing with as many concurrent stressors as economically deprived families. However, they may be moving voluntarily, have greater resources available to them enabling them to cope with these stressors, and they may have developed better coping strategies. All of these are factors affecting how families cope with relocation.

Positive Results of Mobility

Neumerski in an article for Mobility discussed the sixteen-year-old son of a corporate executive who had been relocated five times. As part of a school assignment before his sixth relocation, the young man wrote of his previous moves. His comments overall were positive, saying that through his moves he had learned to become independent and mature, and "to have courage in new and unfamiliar situations" (1994, p. 27). He said that he had become practically a professional at making friends and believed that the moves had brought the family closer together.

Stroh, in her article for Mobility discussing the impact of corporate relocation on teens, said, "these teenagers basically fared very well with their mobile lifestyles. They were typically well adjusted at school, at home, and within the neighborhood" (1993, p. 47).

Pfau, in reporting on her study of 49 junior high school transferring students said, "most of the sample found the experience of relocating to be a positive one" (1990, p. 122).

Schoeni, while discussing many of the difficulties, pain, and losses experienced by relocating families said,

> Relocation can mean new opportunities, higher status, greater job satisfaction, and the excitement of geographic change. It can mean a fresh start with new challenges and new friends, and an opportunity to become involved in civic and local government groups in the new community. It can bring a greater sense of self-awareness, self-reliance, and inner strength. Families can grow closer through their increased awareness and communication with each other. (1991, p. 38)

Discussion

The research from 1990-1995 appears to echo many of the earlier and by now familiar themes. For example, the grief stages continue to be applied to relocation. Frequently mentioned are loss, depression, anomia, gemeinschaft, and the importance of a sense of place and community in people's lives. Other recurring themes are that mobile corporate families are dissatisfied with their social relationships and grieve the loss of their support networks.

Studies continue to show that children suffer the most with frequent moving, particularly adolescents. This seems to be true for corporate as well as the general population. The difference appears to be that corporate children do not suffer academically to the extent that economically deprived children do.

What is new in the 90s is a growing awareness of the linkages between the work and family systems. While the myth of separate worlds has not disappeared, corporations appear to be offering more support to relocating families, and some families with children appear to be more aware of the impact of moving on their children's lives.

What is also new in the 90s is how technology has impacted the family and the workplace. It has changed how families shop, work, and interact. Technology has allowed employees to work from home as never before. Computers, faxes, e-mail, video conferencing, and telecommuting enable employees to stay connected to the workplace and have allowed quality of life to become a reality for many.

The changing family system, the sandwich generation, has also brought a new awareness of how interconnected work and families are. Single parent, dual-career, and non-traditional families are frequently without a support person at home to perform all the necessary tasks following a move. These families are especially vulnerable following a relocation or when an emergency arises. Corporations have responded by changing policies, providing support services, and allowing job sharing and more flexible work schedules.

Relocation in the 90s has also brought an increase in commuter marriages and male relocating partners. Both have been subjected to criticism by society, reflective of society's reluctance to accept the reality of the changing family system. While the family system has been changing, society's perception of gender roles, particularly for women has not kept pace. Dual-career families are continuing to increase and more women are accepting transfers. Gender role stereotyping is evident even within the family when, during relocation, one partner may feel that there is an unfair distribution of the work involved in relocating. This may cause stress in the family system and rupture lines of communication.

What these non-traditional families need to understand is that they are not really separated from society. They are a different form within society and, as they change, their family systems will impact other family systems and society will slowly adjust to the changes. The family system is constantly evolving and more egalitarian family systems in the future may be possible because of the struggles faced by the non-traditional family systems of today.

CHAPTER IX
SUMMARY

And so it is to wanderers of every kind: to the hippie or the traveling salesman. . .to the rising young executive and his wife, or to our ambitious scientists and professionals. The American must look forward, not back. . .for he was born under the sign for the uprooted and homeless, the sign of the wandering star [1]

The purpose of this review was to gain an understanding of the sociological impact of relocation on the family system. The theoretical framework of Systems Theory generated the following questions:

1. Does relocation affect the family system? If so, does it involve the interaction only within the family, or larger societal systems as well?

2. If there are effects, what is the nature of the effects and are they short-term, long-term or both?

The review appears to show that relocation not only impacts the family system but larger societal systems as well, with possible short-term and long-term effects for the family system. These effects impact how family members feel, behave, and interact within the family system as well as how the family interacts with larger societal systems.

[1] The Moving American, George W. Pierson (1973, p. 94).

How Relocation Affects the Family System

Researchers most often describe relocation as a transition involving stages and draw parallels between the relocation process and the grief process. Many factors affect how one adjusts to a relocation. These include perception, culture, age, gender, personality, number of prior moves, concurrent stressors, intra-family structure including their belief system and values, developmental stage, and coping skills. Because relocation is such a complex process no two individuals or families react exactly the same or progress through the stages at exactly the same rate. During this time, like the experience of jet-lag, family members feel dis-oriented and out-of-sync with each other. They are experiencing what is referred to here as Relo-Lag™.

Figure 11. - A traditional family experiencing Relo-Lag™

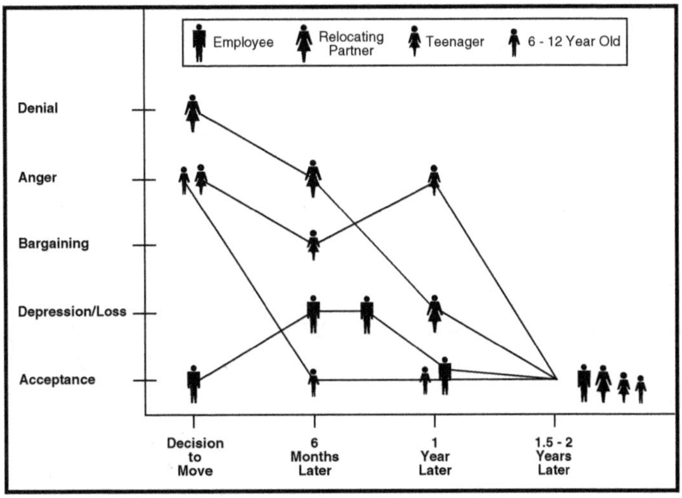

Figure 11 shows how a traditional family might progress through the stages. In this family the relocating partner is female and does not work outside the home. She begins in the denial stage not wanting to believe this is happening. She is happy in her current location, has many friends, and does volunteer work for community groups. She progresses to anger that she does not express (or feel she has a right to) because the move means a big promotion for her husband and is good for his career. The unexpressed anger over her personal losses leads to the depression stage where she remains for about six months. Gradually, as she makes friends in the community, she begins to feel at home. Two years have passed.

The teen, a female, begins in the anger stage. She bargains for an expensive trip back home to spend spring break with her friends and then returns to the anger stage before she finally adjusts.

The younger male child misses his best friend, but after six months makes another friend and makes a good adjustment.

The employee is happy about his promotion. He has some minor setbacks when he realizes that not only is the cost of living much higher in the new location, but the job is not quite what he thought it would be. He does not share these feelings with his family because of guilt, but adjusts well.

From a family systems perspective these typical

reactions by family members create a period of disorganization or Relo-Lag™ during which the family system mobilizes its resources and reorganizes. This period of disorientation and disorganization is the most apparent short-term effect and most researchers believe that, as with the grief stages, this may take as long as two years of adjustment time. Given time and compassionate support, most families progress through the stages and return to their pre-move level of functioning.

A succession of moves may bring about a long-term effect in the family system, causing it to become too tightly closed a system. This may put the family at risk if a crisis occurs, for they will be lacking the outside support necessary to help them through the crisis. For individual family members early research showed that stress brought into the system at this time appeared to affect men and women differently, which some believed was due to early socialization. Men appeared to be at greater risk for heart attacks from work related stress; and women, particularly those who did not work outside the home, were at greater risk for depression.

Children appeared to be at risk if a relocation occurred at certain developmental stages. These are:

– The first individuation stage, ages three to five, when children are in the delicate process of separating from home and are already adjusting their behavior patterns to another authority figure and,

– The second individuation stage, adolescence, from age 13 to 16 when teens are pulling away from their family systems, trying to discover who they are, and where they belong within the larger systems of school and their community.

The teen years are years of great conformity. Placing them in what may feel like an alien environment with different dress codes, hair styles, and behaviors can be extremely confusing to them. Most researchers believe that adolescence presents the most risk when relocating with children. Mention was also made by several researchers of the ages around 9 and 10 when children often make best friends. They believe that a move at this stage could interrupt this process.

For the increasing number of non-traditional families, the dynamics of their family system may be a cause of additional stress during relocation due to a lack of societal support. These include dual-career couples and new family forms which may be single parent, or with a different or same sex partner. In addition, corporations are relocating women employees in greater numbers and there may be a relocating male partner. As the sandwich generation, these families may be relocating with children and an elderly parent.

The more members in the family system, the more complex that the interaction will be as the family progress through the stages of relocation (see Figure 12).

Figure 12. - A sandwich generation family experiencing Relo-Lag™

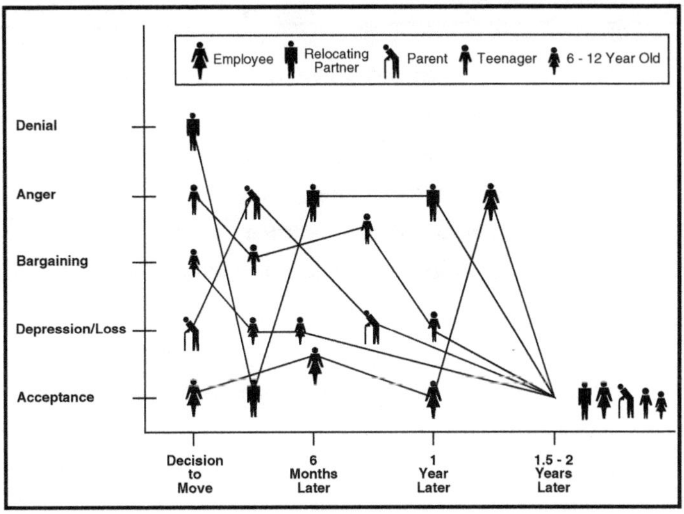

In this dual-career family the relocated employee is female. She is happy with the promotion, misses her colleagues, but appears to be making a quick adjustment. When family members continue to complain months after the move she returns to the anger stage. She resents that she is still expected to play the role of homemaker and nurturer for the family and play the role of boss at work. As the family takes over some of the responsibility at home she returns to the acceptance stage.

The male relocating partner is initially happy for his wife and does not anticipate difficulty in finding a job in the new location. When this does not happen he becomes angry and resentful, especially when friends and family members begin calling him Mr. Mom. When he finds a new position he makes a rapid adjustment.

The elderly parent begins in the depression stage and moves to anger next as he does not like change and feels he has no choice. He returns to depression as he misses his friends and hometown. He gradually adjusts when he discovers a local group of retirees with shared interests.

The teen begins in the anger stage not wanting to leave his friends and new girlfriend. He bargains for a new car, which helps for a time, but returns to the anger stage when he realizes that the new school does not have the ranking of his old one and he might not be able to get into the college of his choice.

The younger child misses her friends but quickly adjusts when the most popular crowd at school seems to accept her.

Both Figure 11 and Figure 12 show the families at the acceptance stage at the end of two years. Rarely is a family system so neat and tidy, and there may be feelings that have been unexpressed that will surface later in time.

Not all families experience relocation negatively. The family may be moving back to a hometown or they may be starting over and trying to leave unhappy memories behind. The family system may be at a stage where all family members are looking forward to the move and progress through the stages with a minimal amount of disruption to the family system. Some moves may bring positive results for all family members.

The Impact of Relocation on Other Systems

Figure 13 illustrates how the family system is connected to the broader systems of work, community, and the nation.

Figure 13. - The interconnection of systems

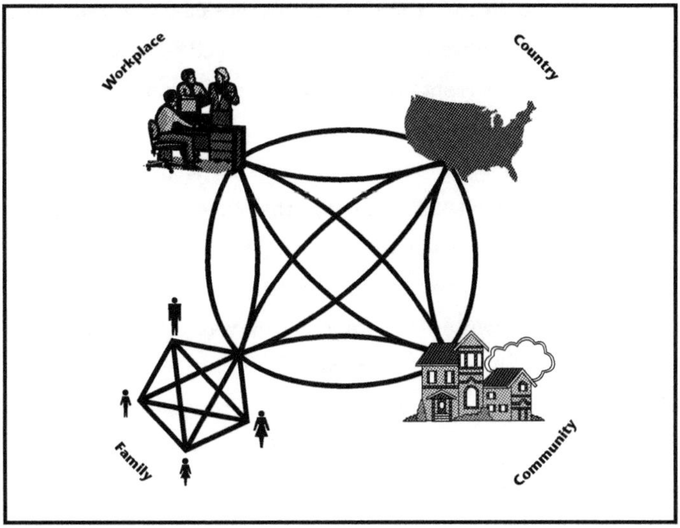

As a system moving through time the family is affected by other systems, just as other systems are affected by the family. As families continually move throughout the United States there is an ebb and flow of interaction that takes place affecting all the systems. Even families that have never moved are affected as friends move away and their communities are changed by relocating families. As each action interacts with the other it is in turn affected by that interaction and that movement creates change throughout all the connecting systems. This change may be thought of in a positive or negative way depending on one's perception.

Limitations of the Review

Qualitative research is the perspective of one researcher. While the goal is always objectivity, material filtered through one individual's perception is always subject to a personal error in judgment. This may cause relevant studies or material to be missed, overlooked, or misinterpreted.

Carol Gilligan (1982) said that the voices left out often highlight what is missing when writing about a subject. The subject of corporate relocation resulted in a review focused on middle class white Americans. This was consistent when all the material for the review was examined. The missing voices are those of people of color, Hispanic, Asian and other minorities who may have quite a different perspective on the corporate relocation experience.

Implications of the Summary

The short-term effect of the disorganization experienced by the family during relocation means that, at a time when good communication is essential for the family, it is most likely to break down. The strong emotions evoked by a serious change in one's life are not always expressed in a calm manner and frequently cause relationships to become strained between family members. This brings stress into the system. From a systems perspective, stress and the breakdown in communication between any members of the family system will affect all the members in that system. In addition, when communication breaks down feelings often go unexpressed. These may include anger and resentment, which may surface at a later date or in some instances lead to depression. Unexpressed anger over the losses associated with relocation was believed by many researchers to be the reason for the depression associated with relocation.

The changing roles of women today may have implications for reduced rates of depression if women feel they are able to express their feelings regarding a relocation. It also appears that women are taking on more roles and may experience more stress due to role overload. The shift from traditional to non-traditional family systems may mean that future stress and depression studies will yield different results than prior studies which indicated higher rates of stress for men and depression for women.

The family system not only has changed over time, but also many of today's relocating families have childcare and eldercare needs simultaneously. Some of these families may be dual-career and single parent families moving without a support person to perform the settling-in tasks. These families may be at risk for additional stress and role overload during relocation.

The implications for children are varied. Very young

children do not have the language skills necessary to express their feelings about a relocation or understand the concepts of distance and permanency. They may feel the loss of a special friend or favorite place but their symptoms are most often expressed somatically. For children in the process of separating from home and adjusting to new authority figures the interruption of this stage may cause a temporary regression to a prior stage. Children may resort to fantasy, denial, withdrawal, or anger, to express their feelings of loss.

For those children whose ages are close to nine and ten, a relocation may disrupt a stage when they often make a best friend. If this process is interrupted, children may find leaving a best friend so painful that they do not wish to risk this pain again. If they have never made a best friend they may not have learned how satisfying it can be.

The adolescent stage was of most concern to researchers who believed that a relocation at this time put teens at risk for developing problems involving their self image as well as their relationships. Adolescence is the second individuation stage when teens are pulling away from the family system and gaining independence. Their ideas of who they are and how they see themselves are formed and reinforced by their peers. Having one image from their previous location, and having to change and adjust this to the new group, is often confusing to them. The star of the football team might move to a location where he might not even make the team. Because local cultures vary greatly across the United States what the main focus and energy of a community is in one area might not rate the back page of the local newspaper in another. These differences can also mean a positive move for some when a teen might have opportunities in the new location that did not exist for them previously.

In an effort to be accepted corporate teens may attempt to win friends by throwing parties, driving a new car, or coaxing their parents to buy them whatever the prized status symbol is among teens in the new town. Parents often give in out of guilt. What is really needed is counseling or a workshop prior to the move so that the family will understand how they might react during a relocation. Counselors who work with corporate families suggest that Brief Solution Focused Therapy may be the most effective approach. Families can be taught strategies and healthy coping behaviors to ease the transition.

The implication of the long-term effect of the family system becoming too tightly closed is that the family may not seek outside help when needed, or accept it when offered. The nuclear family then must deal with all of the stress brought into the family system from the other systems and provide all the emotional and intimacy needs of its members. This places enormous strain and high expectations on a family system already stripped of many of its outside resources.

A closed family system may also make the launching stage of young adults difficult for the family to negotiate.

There has been a resurgence in recent years of single young adults in their twenties and thirties returning home or remaining at home. The reason may be economic but it may also be that the family system is having difficulty negotiating this necessary developmental stage. If this stage is not successfully negotiated, the young adults may never be able to make room in their lives for a partner.

Researchers frequently mention another possible long-term effect for all family members, which is the inability to form close long-term friendships. Families constantly on the move may develop a pattern of forming superficial relationships. While this may be easier on the psyche, it may leave family members feeling that something is missing from their lives. Long term close friendships and relationships are believed to flourish only within the gemeinschaft ideal. These relationships, giving one a sense of belonging and feeling supported by a social network, may be part of what corporate families feel is lacking in their lives. The actual gemeinschaft ideal of living in a small close-knit community may not be compatible with the mobile corporate lifestyle. However, relocating families can be taught not only the importance of opening their family systems, but also how to access needed support from extended family and friends.

The technology that brought the rise of corporate relocation, which separated families, now holds the key to providing ways for families to reconnect. Technology systems and family systems can now interact, enabling families to stay connected around the world.

Suggestions for Corporations and the Family

It is time for Corporations to bury the myth of separate worlds and acknowledge that a relocation affects not only the employee, but also the entire family system. Corporations could provide workshops and counseling about the effects of relocation on the family, preferably before a relocation takes place, in order to help the family decide whether this is a good time for them to relocate. Families would then be aware of the emotional costs when weighing the financial and career benefits of a relocation. Making such workshops and counseling mandatory for all relocating families would remove any stigma of the employee feeling that they might appear weak by requesting outside help.

This type of emotional support appeared to be a real concern on the part of employees who believed they could be putting their careers at risk if they requested assistance. As a result, families must carry some of the responsibility for the lack of support on the part of corporations. By refusing to ask for help they have led some corporations to believe that none is needed.

Finally, while Americans generally appear to be more aware of stress related problems, a relocation is still perceived as an opportunity; the legacy of Americans as an immigrant nation. Each family system is unique and will perceive a relocation differently. However, this perception of moving as opportunity, may leave the family unprepared for the strong emotions and feelings of loss experienced during the move. Counseling can help families clarify their goals and understand the consequences of the choices they make. It can also help them decide if a move at this time will mean danger or opportunity for them.

Suggestions for Future Research

The changing family system and population has implications for future research:

1) Society supported wives moving for their husbands, but does not appear to be as supportive to husbands relocating for their wives. How are these and other non-traditional families adjusting to relocation?

2) Research on corporate relocation has focused on middle class white populations. What is the corporate relocation experience like for people of color and other minority populations?

3) There are indications that a closed family system will have difficulty at the launching stage of the young adults? It would be interesting to compare the launching stage of mobile corporate families with this stage in the general population.

4) Researchers repeatedly mentioned the difficulty that adolescents had developing close relationships after

repeated relocations. Many reports were from parents, and some studies judged the number of friends but not the closeness or intimacy of these friendships. It would be interesting to do a study on this first generation of corporate children who moved as children in the 60s and 70s to see how they experience friendship as adults today.

What Will the Future of Corporate Relocation Be?

Making predictions was popular with many of the writers and researchers who studied mobility. Miller, in 1971 (a period of high vertical mobility) predicted that mobility would become horizontal instead of vertical. The theory behind this, Miller explained, was that as vertical mobility became commonplace and easily attainable, it would lose its appeal and people would look for work they enjoyed and found satisfying. This evolved into the quality of life issues raised at the end of the decade.

In the 80s the future of corporate mobility was frequently discussed. Many predicted the changing family system and the entry of women and minorities into the workplace. They predicted the need for more flexible corporate policies, cross-cultural training, and the rise of technology.

Nemec (1980) said that relocation would always continue, as it was essential to the Human Resource management of corporations. Bastress (1986) agreed and said that even the dual-career couples would continue to relocate because the alternative was job stagnation or unemployment.

A number thought otherwise, such as Bird and Bird (1985) who thought relocation would decrease, as more egalitarian marriages and equal pay would mean fewer wives would be willing to move.

Collie (1984) thought the reason for the decrease would be more telecommuting and working from home. Hermansen (1993) and Jeter (1993) agreed with Collie.

Collie also thought the Sunbelt of the United States would continue to attract mobile families. Glick (1993) agreed that the southern states would be the ones to experience the growth and predicted that by the year 2030 the South would have as many people as the North.

Kanner (1984) thought that this population shift would cause companies to begin relocating to where the people wanted to live, where the climate was pleasant and land costs were low. Quality of life was becoming more important to families than higher wages.

Of course, making predictions only ten years in advance does not have the same kind of visionary appeal, or drama, as some of the earlier predictions. The world changes so fast that many find it difficult to keep up, never mind envision a future for the next generation. Yet, some earlier writers not only attempted to do this but also were amazingly accurate in their predictions.

Toffler in Future Shock wrote that the pessimists tell us that "the family is racing toward oblivion" (1971, p. 238) but the optimists say the family is in for a Golden Age. Toffler predicted that neither would happen but, what was far more likely, was that the family would "breakup, shatter, only to come together in weird and novel ways" (ibid., p. 239). Toffler also forecast that technology would become increasingly sophisticated and advanced and would require an even higher rate of mobility. In order to be able to relocate at this accelerated rate some couples would choose to remain childless. He not only predicted *cloning*, which he said would occur around 1985, but he said that this new invention called a computer would change the way people worked and learned. These computers, Toffler said, would not only enter the classroom but "Human work will move out of the factory and mass office into the community and home" (ibid., p. 402). These predictions were all made over thirty years ago when computers were the size of a room and home computers had not even been invented.

Even earlier, Beach and Beach (1937) did a study "Family migratoriness and child behavior" during the period known as the Great Depression. The term transient is used in the study, they said, to mean simply unsettled or moving versus a stationary family. Beach and Beach stated that a conclusion drawn from the study was that "transiency is not confined at all to the poverty level of society; it is evident also in the middle and upper social strata. Indeed, there seems reason to believe that it may become characteristic of these social layers even more than among the poorer families" (p. 523). That was over sixty years ago and corporate relocation was still in the distant future.

The real future of corporate relocation will be determined by the generation of employees called *baby-busters* by corporate human resource departments. This generation, in their twenties and early thirties, is the first generation of children to grow up with mobility as a way of life. Their parents were focused on careers, and these children were the most involuntary of movers. They experienced first hand; multiple moves, multiple schools and multiple but transient friendships. Will they be willing to move frequently as adults? Will they move their children? Those who had good experiences probably will. Others may remember only painful times and may not. The legacy of moving for opportunity has become incorporated into many corporate family systems. Whether these children see themselves as victims, or stronger for the experience, will determine the future of corporate relocation.

REFERENCES

Acuff, F. L. (1974). Awareness levels of employees considering overseas relocation. Personnel Journal, 53(11), pp. 809-812.

Adams, B. N. (1967). Occupational position, mobility, and the kin of orientation. American Sociological Review, 32(3), pp. 364-377.

Ademec, C. (1982, February 1). Your child's move: How you can make it easier. Army Times, p. 6, p. 8, P. 10, p. 12.

Ahr, P. R. (1987, November-December). Strategies for preventing relocation stress. Mobility, pp. 61-62.

Aldous, J., Osmond, M., & Hicks, M. (1979). Men's work and men's families. In W. Burr, R. Hill, F. I. Nye, & I. Reiss (Eds.), Contemporary theories about the family. New York: The Free Press.

Allen, F. (1981, December 15). Executives' wives describe sources of their contentment, frustration. Wall Street Journal, p. 33.

Allen, F. (1981, December 16). Executives' wives view marriages as combining rewards, sacrifices. Wall Street Journal, p. 29, p. 39.

Allen, F. (1981, December 17). Executives' wives describe effects of husbands' careers on children. Wall Street Journal, p. 27.

Allen, F. (1981, December 18). Wives of executives offer advice to women marrying rising stars. Wall Street Journal, p. 25.

Allen, F. E. (1993, June 21). What problem? Wall Street Journal, p. WF7.

Americans on the move. (1976, March 15). Time, pp. 56-64.

America's new immobile society. (1981, July 27). Business Week, pp. 58-62.

Ammons, P., Nelson, J., & Wodarski, J. (1982). Surviving corporate moves: Sources of stress and adaption among corporate executive families. Family Relations, 31(2), pp. 207-212.

An HR timeline. (1998). Workforce Magazine On-Line. (www.workforceonline.com.), p.1.

Anderson, C., & Stark, C. (1985). Emerging issues from job relocation in the high tech field: Implications for employee assistance programs. Employee Assistance Quarterly, 1(2), pp. 37-54.

Anderson, C., & Stark, C. (1988). Psychosocial problems of job relocation: Preventative roles in industry. Social Work, 33, pp. 38-41.

Anderson, E. A., & Spruill, J. W. (1993). The dual-career family: A lifestyle on the move. In B. H. Settles, D. E. Hanks III, & M. B. Sussman (Eds.), Families on the move: Migration, immigration, emigration, and mobility (pp. 131-147). New York: Haworth.

Anderson, L. S. (1976). When a child begins school. Children Today, 5(4), pp. 16-19.

Andrews, E. L. (1996, December 11). The upper tier of migrant labor. New York Times, p. C1, p. C4.

Angell, R. C. (1936). The family encounters the depression. New York: Charles Scribner's Sons.

Asher, S. J. (1980). Geographic mobility as a factor in adjustment to divorce. Unpublished doctoral dissertation, University of Colorado, Boulder.

Auger, H. J. (1983, September-October). Relocation assistance–Earlier is better. Mobility, pp. 47-49.

Axel, H. (1985). Corporations and families: Changing practices and perspectives (868). New York: The Conference Board.

Baptiste, D. A., Jr. (1993). Immigrant families, adolescents, and acculturation: Insights for therapists. In B. H. Settles, D. E. Hanks III, & M. B. Sussman (Eds.), Families on the move: Migration, immigration, emigration, and mobility (pp. 341-363). New York: Haworth.

Barrett, C. L., & Noble, H. (1973). Mothers' anxieties versus the effects of long distance move on children. Journal of Marriage and the Family, 35, pp. 181-188.

Bartel, A. P. (1979). The migration decision: What role does job mobility play? American Economic Review, 69(5), pp. 775-786.

Bartolomé, F. (1972). Executives as human beings. Harvard Business Review, 50(November-December), pp. 62-69.

Bastress, F. (1986). The new relocating spouse's guide to employment: Options and Strategies in the U.S. and abroad (4th ed.). Manassas Park, Virginia: Impact.

Bayes, M. (1989). The effects of relocation on the trailing spouse. Smith College Studies in Social Work, 59, pp. 280-288.

Beach, A. W., & Beach, W. G. (1937). Family migratoriness and child behavior. Sociology and Social Research, 21(6), pp. 503-523.

Bean, F. D., Bonjean, C. M., & Burton, M. G. (1974). Intergenerational occupational mobility and alienation. Social Forces, 53(1), pp. 62-73.

Beck, R. J., Cohen, S. B., Craik, K. H., Dwyer, M., McCleary, G. F., Jr., & Wapner, S. (1973). Studying environmental moves and relocations. Environment and Behavior, 5(3), pp. 335-349.

Becvar, R. J., & Becvar, D. S. (1982). Systems theory and family therapy. New York: University Press.

Bell, C. (1968). Mobility and the middle class extended family, Sociology (Vol. 2, pp. 172-182). Oxford, UK: Clarendon Press.

Benson, J. (1991, July). A model for a Mobility article. Mobility, p. 14, p. 16.

Benson, J., & Jenkins, L. (1989, August). We survived our relocation, but.... Mobility, pp. 50-52.

Berry, P. J. (1985). The corporate couple. New York: Franklin Watts.

Beshers, J. P., & Laumann, E. O. (1967). Social distance: A network approach. American Sociological Review, 32(2), pp. 225-236.

Bey, D. R., & Lange, J. (1974). Waiting wives: Women under stress. American Journal of Psychiatry, 131(3), pp. 282-286.

Bickerstaffe, G. (1982, March). Have spouse, will travel (if you find us both a job). International Management, pp. 21-22, p. 26.

Bielby, W. T., & Bielby, D. D. (1992). I will follow him: Family ties, gender role beliefs, and reluctance to relocate for a better job. American Journal of Sociology, 97(5), pp. 1241-1267.

Binge, D. (1991, August). Heck no, I won't go! Mobility, pp. 32-35.

Bird, G. A., & Bird, G. W. (1985). Determinants of mobility in two-earner families: Does the wife's income count? Journal of Marriage and the Family, 47, pp. 753-759.

Birtwistle, L. (1992, October). Relocation: A family dilemma. Mobility, pp. 62-63, p. 65.

Blair, J. P., Marchant, K. H., & Medway, F. J. (1984). Aiding the relocated family and mobile child. Elementary School Guidance & Counseling, 18(4), pp. 251-259.

Blau, P. M. (1956). Social mobility and interpersonal relations. American Sociological Review, 21(3), pp. 290-295.

Bloomquist, C. (1982). Employees are more willing to transfer. Personnel Administrator(December), pp. 55-56.

Blotnick, S. (1985, July 29). The new kid on the block. Forbes, p. 214.

Blumberg, L., & Bell, R. R. (1959). Urban migration and kinship ties. Social Problems, 6(4), pp. 328-332.

Bogdan, R. C., & Biklen, S. K. (1992). Qualitative research for education. Boston: Allyn & Bacon.

Boland, E. (1989, August). Relocation stress: Theirs, mine, ours. Mobility, pp. 93-94.

Bonjean, C. M., Bruce, G. D., & Williams Jr., J. A. (1967). Social mobility and job satisfaction: A replication and extension. Social Forces, 45(4), pp. 492-501.

Booth, A. (1979). Does wives' employment cause stress for husbands? Family Coordinator, 28(4), pp. 445-4449.

Borg, W. R., & Gall, M. D. (1989). Educational research. New York: Longman.

Boss, P. G. (1977). A clarification of the concept of psychological father presence in families experiencing ambiguity of boundary. Journal of Marriage and the Family(February), pp. 141-151.

Boss, P. G. (1980). Normative family stress: Family boundary changes across the life-span. Family Relations, 29, pp. 445-450.

Boss, P. G. (1980). The relationship of psychological father presence, wife's personal qualities and wife/family dysfunction in families of missing fathers. Journal of Marriage and the Family(August), pp. 541-549.

Boss, P. G. (1993). The experience of immigration for the mother left behind: The use of qualitative feminist strategies to analyze letters from my Swiss grandmother to my father. In B. H. Settles, D. E. Hanks III, & M. B. Sussman (Eds.), Families on the move: Migration, immigration, emigration, and mobility (pp. 365-378). New York: Haworth.

Boss, P. G., McCubbin, H. I., & Lester, G. (1979). The corporate executive wife's coping patterns in response to routine husband-father absence. Family Process, 18, pp. 79-86.

Bossard, J. (1945). The law of family interaction. In R. J. Becvar & D. S. Becvar (Eds.), Systems theory and family therapy, 1982 (p. 46). New York: University Press.

Bower, E. M. (1967). American children and families in overseas communities. American Journal of Orthopsychiatry, 37(4), pp. 787-796.

Bowlby, J. (1969). Attachment. New York: Basic Books.

Bowlby, J. (1973). Separation. New York: Basic Books.

Bramlage, J. C. (1988). All the right moves: A new strategy for successful relocation. Personnel, 65(5), pp. 40-43.

Breed, B. (1990, November). Spouse employment assistance. Mobility, pp. 45-48.

Breed, W. (1963). Occupational mobility and suicide among white males. American Sociological Review, 28(2), pp. 179-188.

Brenner, B., & Gordon, B. (1991, July). Direct spouse communication: The missing link. Mobility, pp. 55-56, p. 58.

Brett, J. M. (1982). Job transfer and well-being. Applied Psychology, 67(4), pp. 450-463.

Brett, J. M. (1986, May-June). Why employees relocate. Mobility, pp. 17-23.

Brett, J. M., & Reilly, A. H. (1988). On the road again: Predicting the job transfer decision. Applied Psychology, 73(4), pp. 614-620.

Brett, J. M., & Stroh, L. K. (1995). Willingness to relocate internationally. Human Resource Management, 34(3), pp. 405-424.

Brett, J. M., Stroh, L. K., & Reilly, A. H. (1990). Impact of societal shifts and corporate changes on employee relocation. Washington: Employee Relocation Council.

Brett, J. M., & Werbel, J. D. (1980, November-December). Building an understanding of relocation. Mobility, pp. 7-11.

Bridges, W. (1980). Transitions. Boston: Addison-Wesley.

Brienza, A. M. (1994, May). Thirty years of excellence. Mobility, pp. 35-40, p. 42, p. 44.

Brody, E. B. (1969). Migration and adaption: The nature of the problem. American Behavioral Scientist, 13(1), pp. 5-13.

Brown, G. W. (1984). Contextual measures of life events. In B. S. Dohrenwend & B. P. Dohrenwend (Eds.), Stressful life events & their contexts (pp. 187-201). New Brunswick: Rutgers University Press.

Brown, G. W., Bhrolchain, M., & Harris, T. (1975). Social class and psychiatric disturbance among women in an urban population. Sociology, 9, pp. 225-254.

Brown, P. L. (1997, May 25). Reliving myth of the presidential log cabin. New York Times, p. 1, p. 6.

Bruzzese, A. (1994, June 3). All the right moves. Human Resource Executive, pp. 49-52.

Bryson, J. B., & Bryson, R. (Eds.). (1978). Dual-career couples: A special issue of psychology of women quarterly. New York: Human Sciences Press.

Buckley, J. (1989, January 16). The new organization man. U.S. News & World Report, pp. 41-43.

Burchinal, L. G. (1963). Do family moves harm children. Iowa Farm Science, 17(9), pp. 11-12.

Burke, R. J. (1974). Personnel job transfers: Some data and recommendations. Studies in Personnel Psychology, 6(1), pp. 35-46.

Burr, W. R. (1973). Theory construction and the sociology of the family. New York: John Wiley and Sons.

Business Bulletin-Employee transfers. (1977, July 28). Wall Street Journal, p. 1.

Butler, E. W., McAllister, R. J., & Kaiser, E. J. (1973). The effects of voluntary and involuntary residential mobility on females and males. Journal of Marriage and the Family, 35, pp. 219-227.

Capell, P. (1996, February 26). Staying put: The right move. The Wall Street Journal, pp. R6-R7.

Caplan, G., & Killilea, M. (Eds.). (1976). Support systems and mutual help: Multidisciplinary explorations. New York: Grune & Stratton.

Cardwell, J. W. (1980). The other side of relocation-Relocating the spouse. Personnel Administrator, 25(9), pp. 53-57.

Carter, B., & McGoldrick, M. (1989). The changing family life cycle. Boston: Allyn & Bacon.

Carter, B. D. (1981). Family stress and social adjustment following geographic relocation: A study of the function of organizational policy and social network supports. (Doctoral dissertation, University of Virginia). University Microfilms International No. 8228655 (1996).

Catalyst's women in corporate leadership study. (1998). PBS On-Line Newshour - On-line Forum. (www.pbs.org), p.1.

Center for Agricultural and Economic Development. (1965). Family mobility in our dynamic society. Ames: Iowa State University Press.

Cetron, M. (1986, Fall Workshop Issue). Relocation: Looking to the future. Mobility, pp. 53-54.

Cetron, M. J. (1987, Spring Conference Issue). Dual income families and their effect on employee mobility. Mobility, pp. 52-53, pp. 55-56.

Cetron, M. J. (1993, October). The relocating work force of the future. Mobility, pp. 73-74, p. 76.

Cetron, M. J., Lucken, R., McFadden, C. F., & Weir, B. J. (1987). Impact of the changing family on employee relocation. Washington: Employee Relocation Council.

Changing 45 million jobs. (1981, August 3). Business Week, pp. 62-63, pp. 66-67.

Chapman, F. S. (1987, February 16). Executive guilt: Who's taking care of the children? Fortune, pp. 30-37.

Chesteen, H. E., Jr., Bergeron, V., & Addison, W. P. (1970). Geographic mobility and mental disorder. Hospital and Community Psychiatry, 21(January), pp. 43-44.

Chesters, A. (1990, July). Developing nomadic executives. Mobility, pp. 31-34.

Chudacoff, H. P. (1972). Mobile Americans. New York: Oxford University Press.

Clark, R. H., & Vennard, K. B. (1983, September-October). Relocation and stress. Mobility, pp. 15-17.

Clark, W. A. V., & Moore, E. G. (1982). Residential mobility and public programs: Current gaps between theory and practice. Journal of Social Issues, 38(3), pp. 35-50.

Clayton, P., Desmarais, L., & Winoker, G. (1968). A study of normal bereavement. American Journal of Psychiatry, 125(2), pp. 168-178.

Collie, H. C. (1984, July-August). Projections for relocation in the year 2003. Mobility, pp. 14-16.

Collie, H. C. (1988, September-October). The big picture. Mobility, pp. 4-8.

Collie, H. C. (1990, November). Relocation trends: Forecasting the 1990s. Mobility, pp. 17-19.

Collie, H. C. (1991, May). The importance of mobility: A business necessity, a personal hardship. Mobility, p. 97.

Collie, H. C., & DiDomenico, P. J. (1980). Relocation trends–moving into the 80's. Personnel Administrator, 25(9), pp. 31-35, pp. 66-68.

Conklin, B. (1991, November). The story of a single parent transferee. Mobility, pp. 33-34.

Constable, R. T. (1978). Mobile families and the school. Social Casework, 59(7), pp. 419-427.

Cooper, C. L., & Payne, R. (Eds.). (1980). Current concerns in occupational stress. New York: John Wiley & Sons.

Cornille, T. A. (1993). Support systems and the relocation process for children and families. In B. H. Settles, D. E. Hanks III, & M. B. Sussman (Eds.), Families on the move: Migration, immigration, emigration, and mobility (pp. 281-298). New York: Haworth.

Cornille, T. A., Bayer, A. E., & Smyth, C. K. (1983). Schools and newcomers: A national survey of innovative programs. Personnel and Guidance Journal, 62(4), pp. 229-236.

Cornille, T. A., & Brotherton, W. D. (1993). Applying the developmental family therapy model to issues of migrating families. In B. H. Settles, D. E. Hanks III, & M. B. Sussman (Eds.), Families on the move: Migration, immigration, emigration, and mobility (pp. 325-340). New York: Haworth.

Corporate woman: Now eager to accept transfers. (1980, May 26). Business Week, p. 153, p. 156.

Costello, J. (1976). Why more managers are refusing transfers. Nation's Business, 64(10), pp. 4-5.

Crabbs, M. A., & Crabbs, S. K. (1980). New kid on the block: How one district extends a helping hand. National Elementary Principal, 59(4), pp. 42-45.

Cramer, W., & Dorsey, S. (1970). Are movers losers? Elementary School Journal(April), pp. 387-390.

Crane, K. (1991, February 4). Making a move painless and inexpensive. Computerworld, p. 78.

Crosby, M., & Nightingale, A. (1986, May-June). The trailing male spouse. Mobility, p. 36.

Crosby, M. A. (1985, May-June). Survey of Fortune 500 companies on spouse career assistance. Mobility, pp. 79-82.

Cuber, J. F., & Harroff, P. B. (1965). The significant Americans: A study of sexual behavior among the affluent. New York: Appleton-Century.

Culbert, S. A., & Renshaw, J. R. (1972). Coping with the stresses of travel as an opportunity for improving the quality of work and family life. Family Process, 11, pp. 321-337.

Curtis, B., & Vossler, M. (1986, March-April). Child care and relocation. Mobility, pp. 69-71.

Curtis, R. F. (1960). Income and occupational mobility. American Sociological Review, 25(5), pp. 727-730.

Cushmir, L. H. (1986). Increasing women's job commitment: Some practical answers. Personnel, 63(1), pp. 41-44.

Dail, P. W. (1993). Homelessness in America: Involuntary family migration. In B. H. Settles, D. E. Hanks III, & M. B. Sussman (Eds.), Families on the move: Migration, immigration, emigration, and mobility (pp. 55-75). New York: Haworth.

DaVanzo, J. (1977). Why families move: A model of the geographic mobility of married couples. U.S. Department of Labor, R & D Monograph 48. Washington, DC: U.S. Government Printing Office.

David, H. P., & Elkind, D. (1966). Family adaptation overseas. Mental Hygiene, 50, pp. 92-99.

Davis, T. B. (1986, November-December). 20001–a relocation odyssey. Mobility, p. 37, pp. 40-41, p. 43, p. 46.

Day, R. (1984). Recent directions in life stress research from a public health perspective. In B. S. Dohrenwend & B. P. Dohrenwend (Eds.), Stressful life events & their contexts (pp. 281-285). New Brunswick: Rutgers University Press.

de Alba, R., & Byrnes, B. (1983, September-October). Employee relocation–Some new findings on adjustment and productivity. Mobility, p. 51, pp. 53-54.

Dean, D. G. (1961). Alienation: Its meaning and measurement. American Sociological Review, 26(5), pp. 753-757.

DeJong, G. F. (1977). Residential preferences and migration. Demography, 14, pp. 169-178.

Delatiner, B. (1984, April). Trailing a transferred husband. Working Mother, pp. 70-71, p. 75.

Dever, S. (1980). Relocation–executive style. Personnel Administrator, 25(9), pp. 63-64, pp. 104-105.

Dickinson, J. (1988). Complete guide to family relocation. Lake Oswego, Oregon: Wheatherstone.

Dickson, P. W. (1995, July). Effects of moving. Mobility, pp. 51-54.

Dickson, P. W. (1995, July). Maybe it should be called 'dislocation'.... Mobility, pp. 51-52, p. 54.

Dickson, P. W. (1995, November). Kids are transferees, too. Mobility, pp. 47-48.

Dohrenwend, B. S., & Dohrenwend, B. P. (Eds.). (1984). Stressful life events & their contexts. (Vol. 2). New Brunswick: Rutgers University Press.

Donohue, J. G. (1983, November-December). Working with the corporate transferee. Mobility, pp. 61-62.

Donohue, K. C., & Gullotta, T. P. (1981, November-December). FIT: What corporations can do to ease relocation stress. Mobility, pp. 53-57.

Donohue, K. C., & Gullotta, T. P. (1983). The coping behavior of adolescents following a move. Adolescence, 18(70), pp. 391-401.

Doull, S., & Rose, E. (1986, March-April). Making the first move: Initiating spouse programs. Mobility, p. 49.

Downie, N. M. (1953). A comparison between children who have moved from school with those who have been in continuous residence on various factors of adjustment. Journal of Educational Psychology, 44, pp. 51-53.

Dransfield, A. (1984, August 20). The uneasy life of the corporate spouse. Fortune, pp. 27-32.

Driessnack, C. H. (1982). Spouse relocation: Creative approach to recruitment and employee transfer. Personnel Administrator(December), pp. 59-60, p. 62, p. 64.

Driskell, P. (1988). Cut moving costs without sacrificing service. Personnel Journal(May), pp. 111-113.

Drushal, J. G. (1973). On becoming non-strangers. Personnel Administrator(January-February), pp. 18-20.

Duhl, L. J. (1963). The urban condition. New York: Basic Books.

Duncan, B. (1956). Factors in work-residence separation: Wage and salary workers. Sociology, 21(1), pp. 48-57.

Duncan, G. J., & Newman, S. (1975). People as planners: The fulfillment of residential mobility expectations. In G. J. Duncan & J. N. Morgan (Eds.), Five thousand American families: Patterns of economic progress. Ann Arbor: Institute for Social Research.

Duncan, R. P., & Perrucci, C. C. (1976). Dual occupation families and migration. American Sociological Review, 41(April), pp. 252-261.

Dunn, D. H. (1985, February 4). Cushioning the shocks of job relocation. Business Week, pp. 89-90.

Durkheim, E. (1947). The division of labor in society. New York: The Free Press of Glencoe.

Echikson, R. (1983, November-December). Relocating dual career families: Critical issue in today's labor market. Mobility, pp. 65-66.

Edstrom, A., & Galbraith, J. R. (1977). Transfer of managers as a coordination and control strategy in multinational organizations. Administrative Science Quarterly, 22, pp. 248-263.

Eisner, E. W., & Peshkin, A. (1990). Qualitative inquiry in education. New York: Teachers College.

Ekland, B. K. (1965). Academic ability, higher education, and occupational mobility. American Sociological Review, 30(10), pp. 735-746.

Ellis, R. A., & Lane, W. C. (1963). Structural supports for upward mobility. American Sociological Review, 28(3), pp. 743-756.

Ellis, R. A., & Lane, W. C. (1967). Social mobility and social isolation: A test of Sorkin's dissociative hypothesis. American Sociological Review, 32(2), pp. 237-256.

Erkut, S. (1986, January-February). Coping with teenagers' resistance to moving. Mobility, pp. 39-40, p. 43.

Ervin, T. B. (1983, November-December). Twenty years of helping the transferee. Mobility, pp. 14-15.

Estrin, D. (1986, May-June). Taking the hassle out of relocation. Mobility, pp. 59-60.

Evans, J. W., Jr. (1966). The effect of pupil mobility upon academic achievement. National Elementary Principal, 45(5), pp. 18-22.

Evans, L. A. (1980, May-June). Spouse placement: Relocating a dual career family. Mobility, pp. 51-53.

Evans, P., & Bartolomé, F. (1981). Must success cost so much. New York: Basic Books.

Fairchild, H. M., & Tucker, M. B. (1982). Black residential mobility: Trends and characteristics. Journal of Social Issues, 38(3), pp. 51-75.

Fanning, D. (1990, April 8). When she moves, and he must trail along. The New York Times, p. 29.

Fasano, K. (1995, August). Dealing with people who are dealing with relocation stress. Mobility.

Fava, S. F. (1956). Suburbanism as a way of life. Sociology, 21(1), pp. 34-37.

Feitler-Karchin, B. J., & Getting, K. (1987, January-February). Trailing spouse issues: Easing transitional stress. Mobility, pp. 59-62.

Feldbaum, C. L., Christenson, T. E., & O'Neal, E. C. (1980). An observational study of the assimilation of the newcomer to preschool. Child Development, 51, pp. 497-507.

Fellin, P., & Litwak, E. (1963). Neighborhood cohesion under conditions of mobility. American Sociological Review, 28(3), pp. 364-376.

Felmlee, D. H. (1982). Womens' job mobility processes within and between employers. American Sociological Review, 47, pp. 142-151.

Felsten, G. J. (1981). Current considerations in plant shutdowns and relocations. Personnel Journal, 60(6), pp. 369-372.

Ferber, M., & Huber, J. (1979). Husbands, wives, and careers. Journal of Marriage and the Family, 41(2), pp. 315-325.

Fields, J. P. (1983, March-April). Meeting the challenge of relocation resistance. Mobility, p. 53, pp. 55-56.

Fisher, J. L. (1993). Effects of immigration reform and control act on families. In B. H. Settles, D. E. Hanks III, & M. B. Sussman (Eds.), Families on the move: Migration, immigration, emigration, and mobility (pp. 233-239). New York: Haworth.

Fisher, M., & Greenberg, C. (1983, March-April). Families find forums to solve relocation problems. Mobility, pp. 63-64.

Flanagan, W. G., & Bamford, J. (1983, November 21). More than a moving experience. Forbes, p. 310, p. 312.

Flynn, G. (1996). Heck no–we won't go! Personnel Journal(March), pp. 37-43.

Foegen, J. H. (1977). If it means moving, forget it? Personnel Journal(August), pp. 414-416.

Foltz, R. G. (1980). Relocation communications. Personnel Administrator, 25(9), p. 14.

For lots of reasons more workers are saying "no" to job transfers. (1977, February 14). U.S. News & World Report, pp. 73-74.

Ford, J. D., & Ford, J. G. (1986). A systems theory analysis of employee assistance programs. Employee Assistance Quarterly, 2(1), pp. 37-48.

Ford, R. (1995, November 26). Running in place. New York Times, p. 11.

Foster, L. W., & Liebrenz, M. L. (1977). Corporate moves–Who pays the psychic costs? Personnel(November-December), pp. 67-75.

Foster, R. G. (1956). Effect of mobility on the family. American Journal of Public Health, 46(7), pp. 813-818.

Fowler, E. M. (1977, November 11). Helping the transferred employee. New York Times, p. 72.

Frankel, M., & Strauss, N. (1981, May-June). Family concerns: A threat to corporate relocation. Mobility, p. 20, p. 22.

Fried, M. (1982). Residential attachment: Sources of residential and community satisfaction. Journal of Social Issues, 38(3), pp. 107-119.

Friedman, H. B. (1989). Psychological assessment of the effects of job transfers on executives and their families. (Doctoral dissertation, The University of Michigan). University Microfilms International No. 9001628 (1995).

Friedrich, B., & Hultstrand, S. (1978). Did somebody pack the baby? Englewood Cliffs, New Jersey: Prentice-Hall.

Fuchs, R. (1971). Different meanings of employment for women. Human Relations, 24(6), pp. 495-499.

Fusco, M. A. C. (1990). With American businesses paying twenty billion dollars a year for moving costs, employee relocation has become a hot topics for the 1990s. Employment Relations Today, 17, pp. 79-83.

Gans, H. J. (1967). The Levittowners. New York: Pantheon.

Gardiner, C. V., & Rich, K. L. (1980). Relocation policies: Boom and bust. Personnel Administrator, 25(9), pp. 37-41, p. 64, p. 104.

Gaylord, M. (1979). Relocation and the corporate family: Unexplored issues. Social Work, 24, pp. 186-191.

Gaylord, M., & Symons, E. (1986). Relocation stress: A definition and a need for services. Employee Assistance Quarterly, 2(1), pp. 31-36.

Gerstel, N., & Gross, H. E. (1982). Commuter marriages: A review, Marriage and family review (pp. 71-93). New York: Haworth.

Giammattei, H., & Slaughter, K. (1970). Help your family make a better move. Garden City, New York: Doubleday.

Gilligan, C. (1982). In a different voice: Psychological theory and women's development. Cambridge, Massachusetts: Harvard University Press.

Gilliland, C. H. (1967). The relation of pupil mobility to achievement in elementary school. *Journal of Experimental Education, 35*, pp.74-80.

Gilliland, N. C. (1979). The problem of geographic mobility for dual career families. *Journal of Comparative Family Studies, 10*(3), pp. 346-358.

Glass, D. C. (1977). Stress, behavior patterns, and coronary disease. *American Science, 65*, pp. 177-187.

Glick, P. C. (1993). The impact of geographic mobility on individuals and families, *Marriage and family review* (Vol. 19, pp. 31-54). New York: Haworth.

Glueck, W. F. (1974). Managers: Mobility and morale. *Business Horizons, 17*(6), pp. 65-70.

Glynn, B. L. (1981, March-April). A funny thing happened on the way to my new location. *Mobility,* pp. 61-63.

Golden, R. R., & Dohrenwend, B. S. (1984). A path analytic method for testing casual hypotheses about the life stress process. In B. S. Dohrenwend & B. P. Dohrenwend (Eds.), *Stressful life events & their contexts* (pp. 258-277). New Brunswick: Rutgers University Press.

Gordon, R. E., & Gordon, K. K. (1958). Emotional disorders of children in a rapidly growing suburb. *International Journal of Social Psychiatry, 4*(2), pp. 85-97.

Gordon, S. (1976). *Lonely in America*. New York: Simon & Schuster.

Gore, S. (1984). Stress-buffering functions of social supports: An appraisal and clarification of research models. In B. S. Dohrenwend & B. P. Dohrenwend (Eds.), *Stressful life events & their contexts* (pp. 202-221). New Brunswick: Rutgers University Press.

Gorran, G. M. (1994, May). Corporate expectations in relocation. *Mobility,* pp. 115-116, p. 118.

Gottman, J. M. (1977). Toward a definition of social isolation in children. *Child Development, 48*(2), pp. 513-517.

Gottschalk, E., C., Jr. (1982, January 21). Firms increasingly help spouses of transferred employees find jobs. Wall Street Journal, p. 21.

Govaerts, K. (1985). To work and to love: An examination of vocational and marital satisfaction in the dual-career marriage. Unpublished doctoral dissertation, University of Nebraska, Lincoln.

Greene, J. E., Sr., & Daughty, S. L. (1961). Factors associated with school mobility. The Journal for Educational Sociology, 35(September), pp. 36-40.

Greenwald, D. (1987). Coping with moving. New York: Rosen.

Gregory, J. (1982, January-February). Employees overcome relocation-related problems: Case studies. Mobility, pp. 45-47.

Grindlinger, S. (1993, April). An antidote for overpayment angst. Mobility, pp. 40-41.

Gross, H. (1980). Dual career couples who live apart: Two types. Journal of Marriage and the Family, 42, pp. 567-576.

Gross, T. S. (1981). Blueprint for a group move. Personnel Journal(July), pp. 546-547.

Gross, T. S. (1987, Fall Workshop Issue). A look ahead: Relocation management in the 90's. Mobility, p. 5, p. 9, p. 11, p. 13.

Guillet, D. R. (1980). Getting your employees to relocate–When they won't. Administrative Management, 41(10), pp. 43-44, p. 70, p. 73-74.

Gullotta, T. P., & Donohue, K. C. (1981). Corporate families: Implications for prevention intervention. Social Casework, 62(2), pp. 106-114.

Gullotta, T. P., & Donohue, K. C. (1981). The corporate family: Theory and treatment. Journal of Marital and Family Therapy(April), pp. 151-158.

Gullotta, T. P., & Donohue, K. C. (1982). Preventing family distress during relocation: Initiatives for human resource managers. Personnel Administrator(December), pp. 37-43.

Gullotta, T. P., Stevens, S. J., Donohue, K. C., & Clark, V. S. (1981). Adolescents in corporate families. Adolescence, 16(63), pp. 621-628.

Hagel, R. (1992, July). Employee mobility: An important part of the business playbook. Mobility, pp. 46-48, p. 49.

Haggai, T. S. (1981, July-August). A real world perspective of employee relocation. Mobility, pp. 9-10.

Handzel, P. R., & Turici, M. (1982, May-June). Transfer trauma: A community college concern. Mobility, pp. 11-12, pp. 15-16.

Hanks III, D. E., & Liprie, M. L. (1993). South African migration and the effects on the family. In B. H. Settles, D. E. Hanks III, & M. B. Sussman (Eds.), Families on the move: Migration, immigration, emigration, and mobility (pp. 175-192). New York: Haworth.

Hanks, R. S., & Sussman, M. B. (1993). Rethinking family/organization linkage in job-related transfers. In B. H. Settles, D. E. Hanks III, & M. B. Sussman (Eds.), Families on the move: Migration, immigration, emigration, and mobility (pp. 99-111). New York: Haworth.

Hanna III, H. W. (1985, January-February). Meeting all relocation needs of corporate clients. Mobility, pp. 31-32.

Hansen, K. A. (1996). Geographical mobility: March 1993 to March 1994. Washington: U.S. Department of Commerce, Bureau of Census.

Hareven, T. K. (1982). American families in transition: Historical perspectives on change. In F. Walsh (Ed.), Normal family processes (1st ed., pp. 446-466). New York: Guilford.

Harris, M. (1987, May). Relocation: Relieving the bulk of the burden. Mortgage Banking, p. 93, p. 95.

Harrison, R., & Rich, K. L. (1984, March-April). Healing the pain of relocation. Mobility, pp. 23-26.

Hazelrigg, L. E. (1974). Occupational mobility in nineteenth-century U.S. cities: A review of some evidence. Social Forces, 53(1), pp. 21-32.

Heckman, N. A., Bryson, R., & Bryson, J. (1977). Problems of professional couples: A content analysis. Journal of Marriage and the Family, 39, pp. 323-330.

Helzer, J. E. (1984). Methodological issues in the interpretations of the consequences of extreme situations. In B. S. Dohrenwend & B. P. Dohrenwend (Eds.), Stressful life events & their contexts (pp. 108-129). New Brunswick: Rutgers University Press.

Hendershott, A. P. (1989). Residential mobility, social support and adolescent self-concept. Adolescence, 24(93), pp. 217-232.

Hendershott, A. P. (1995). Moving for work. Lanham, Maryland: University Press.

Herman, J. B., & Werbel, J. (1978). The effect of job transfer on employees and their families: Baseline survey report. Washington: Employee Relocation Council.

Hermansen, M. F. (1993, August). Relocation 1999. Mobility, p. 40, pp. 43-44.

Herring, L. (1988). Momentum: Book 1. Saint Louis: The Impact Group.

Herring, L. (1988, May-June). The psychology of a positive relocation. Mobility, pp. 15-17.

Herring, L. (1989). Helping spouses helps employers. Personnel Journal, 68(1), pp. 35-37.

Herring, L. (1995, October). One family's relocations. Mobility, pp. 77-78, p. 80.

Herring, L., & Greenwood, P. (1995, July). A mid-year relocation...What will happen to the children. Mobility, pp. 48-50.

Herring, L., & Suarez, J. (1994, July). 'Sandwich generation' transferees face tough decisions. Mobility, pp. 51-53.

Hetherington, E. M. (1972). Effects of father absence on personality development in adolescent daughters. Developmental Psychology, 7(3), pp. 313-326.

Hill, R. (1958). Generic features of families under stress. Social Casework, 39, pp. 139-149.

Hodge, R. W., & Treiman, D. J. (1966). Occupational mobility and attitude toward Negroes. American Sociological Review, 31(1), pp. 93-102.

Hogue, B. (1990, December). Relocation in the 1990s–One opinion. Mobility, pp. 37-38.

Holland-Jacobsen, S., Holland, R. P., & Cook, A. S. (1984). Mobility: Easing the transition for students. The School Counselor, 32(1), pp. 49-53.

Hollingshead, A. B., Ellis, R., & Kirby, E. (1954). Social mobility and mental illness. American Sociological Review, 19(5), pp. 577-584.

Holloman, J. (1985, July-August). Identifying and dealing with employee stress. Mobility, p. 57.

Holloman, J. (1990, January). Assisting the family in the '90s. Mobility, pp. 25-28.

Holloman, J. (1991, January). Hot topics in relocation. Mobility, pp. 16-21.

Holmes, T. H., & Rahe, R. H. (1967). The social readjustment rating scale. (Vol. 2). Oxford, United Kingdom: Pergamon.

Holmstrom, L. (1972). The two career family. (Vol. 2). Cambridge, Massachusetts: Schenkman.

Holston, J. E. (1989, December). The end of a decade of moving. Mobility, pp. 14-21.

Horan, P. M. (1974). The structure of occupational mobility: Conceptualization and analysis. Social Forces, 53(1), pp. 33-45.

Horowitz, R. (1993). The power of ritual in a Chicano community: A young woman's status and expanding family ties. In B. H. Settles, D. E. Hanks III, & M. B. Sussman (Eds.), Families on the move: Migration, immigration, emigration, and mobility (pp. 257-280). New York: Haworth.

House, J. S. (1974). Occupational stress and coronary disease: A review and theoretical integration. Journal of Health and Social Behavior, 15, pp. 12-27.

Houseknecht, S. K., & Macke, A. S. (1981). Combining marriage and career: The marital adjustment of professional women. Journal of Marriage and the Family, 43,(August), pp. 651-661.

How would you like to move...again. (1963, April 19). Sales Management,90, pp. 93-94.

Howard, C. G. (1973). Is your manager suitable for overseas assignment? Personnel Administrator(January-February), pp. 25-28.

Huggins, J. (1973). Taking the trauma out of transfers. Personnel Administrator(January-February), pp. 21-22.

Hutchison, I. W. (1982, November-December). Relocating families with adolescents. Mobility, pp. 47-49.

Hutton, J. B., Roberts, T. G., Walker, J., & Zuniga, J. (1987). Ratings of severity of life events by ninth-grade students. Psychology in the Schools, 24, pp. 63-68.

Hyman, M. R. (1984). A study of geographic mobility and motility as they relate to marketing. Unpublished doctoral dissertation, Purdue University, West Lafayette.

Imber-Black, E. (1988). Families and larger systems. New York: Guilford.

Imundo, L. V., Jr. (1974). Problems associated with managerial mobility. Personnel Journal, 53(12), pp. 910-914.

Isabella, L. A., & Ornstein, S. (1988). Getting and giving the hidden messages on relocation. Personnel, 65(3), pp. 30-36.

Jaco, E. G., & Belknap, I. (1953). Is a new family form emerging in the urban fringe? American Sociological Review, 18(5), pp. 551-557.

Jalongo, M. R. (1985). When young children move. Young Children, 40, pp. 51-58.

Janik, C. (1988). Positive moves. New York: Weidenfeld & Nicholson.

Janowitz, M. (1967). The community press in an urban setting (2nd ed.). Chicago: University of Chicago Press.

Jenkins, C. D., Zyzanski, S. J., & Rosenman, R. H. (1976). Risk of new myocardial infarction in middle-aged men with manifest coronary heart disease. Circulation, 53, pp. 342-347.

Jennings, E. E. (1967). The mobile manager: A study of the new generation of top executives: The University of Michigan.

Jensen, N., Copans, S., & McCollum, A. (1995, October). Children on the move: How can relocation professionals help? Mobility, pp. 31-32, p. 34, p. 36, p. 38.

Jeter, K. (1993). Wedding rings and take out food: Early human mobility ritualized in later human pilgrimage. In B. H. Settles, D. E. Hanks III, & M. B. Sussman (Eds.), Families on the move: Migration, immigration, emigration, and mobility (pp. 379-400). New York: Haworth.

Johnson, A. A. (1990). Relocating two-earner couples: What companies are doing (247). New York: The Conference Board.

Johnson, J. B. (1981, May-June). Educational counseling: A relocation service. Mobility, p. 32, p. 34, p. 36.

Johnson, L. (1991, October). Managerial women and relocation. Mobility, pp. 47-48, p. 50.

Jones, A. P., & Demaree, R. G. (1975). Family disruption, social indices, and problem behavior: A preliminary study. Journal of Marriage and the Family(August), pp. 497-502.

Jones, S. B. (1973). Geographic mobility as seen by the wife and mother. Journal of Marriage and the Family, 35, pp. 210-218.

Jones, S. F. (1984, September-October). It's your move: Coping with relocation. Mobility, p. 81, p. 83, p. 85.

Jordan, D. H. (1995, January). Family issues-On the edge of the century. Mobility, pp. 57-60.

Juhasz, A. M., & Plazas, C. A. (1993). The impossible dream: Education for the integration of Hispanic families. In B. H. Settles, D. E. Hanks III, & M. B. Sussman (Eds.), Families on the move: Migration, immigration, emigration, and mobility (pp. 311-323). New York: Haworth.

Jurich, A. P., Collins, O. P., & Griffen, C. (1993). Coping with the displaced farm family: The new rural migration. In B. H. Settles, D. E. Hanks III, & M. B. Sussman (Eds.), Families on the move: Migration, immigration, emigration, and mobility (pp. 77-98). New York: Haworth.

Kahnweiler, J. B. (1988, March-April). The human side of relocation. Mobility, pp. 56-58, p. 60.

Kaminsky, C. (1982, November-December). Would you accept this relocation? Mobility, pp. 53-55.

Kanner, R. (1984, May-June). The changing personality of relocation: Different players, different places. Mobility, pp. 77-78.

Kanter, R. M. (1977). Men and women of the corporation. New York: Basic Books.

Kantor, M. B. (Ed.). (1963). Mobility and mental health: Proceedings of the fifth annual conference on community health research, Social Science Institute, Washington University, St. Louis. Springfield, Illinois: Charles C. Thomas.

Kaplan, H. B. (1983). Psychosocial stress: Trends in theory and research. New York: Academic.

Kaplan, L. (1978). Oneness and separateness: From infant to individual. New York: Simon & Schuster.

Kaplan, M. F., & Glenn, A. (1978). Women and the stress of moving: A self-help approach. Social Casework(July 1978), pp. 434-436.

Kasarda, J., & Janowitz, M. (1974). Community attachment in mass society. American Sociological Review, 39, pp. 328-339.

Keith, P. M., & Schafer, R. B. (1980). Role strain and depression in two-job families. Family Relations, 29, pp. 483-488.

Kelley, K. (1995, May). 'Trailing' no more! Mobility, pp. 93-95.

Kessin, K. (1971). Social and psychological consequences of intergenerational occupational mobility. American Journal of Sociology, 77(1), pp. 1-18.

Kiechel III, W. (1987, April 13). When the boss wants you to move. Fortune, p. 125, p. 128.

Kilpatrick, A. C. (1982). Job changes in dual-career families: Danger or opportunity? Family Relations, 31(3), pp. 363-368.

King, M. (1996, June 2). A stress-free moving day. St. Louis Post Dispatch, p. G1.

Koerber, S. M. (1988, January-February). Selecting a relocation management company. Mobility, pp. 61-62.

Koerber, S. M. (1988, March-April). Meeting the challenge of the 1980: Servicing corporate relocation. Mobility, pp. 87-89.

Koerber, S. M. (1988, May-June). Selecting a relocation management company: 'The Answer'. Mobility, p. 37, p. 39.

Kolkind, M. (1991, January). Just say 'yes' to a move in the '90s. Mobility, pp. 48-50.

Kosko, B. (1993). Fuzzy thinking: The new science of fuzzy logic. New York: Hyperion.

Kouri, K. M., & Lasswell, M. (1993). Black-white marriages: Social change and intergenerational mobility. In B. H. Settles, D. E. Hanks III, & M. B. Sussman (Eds.), Families on the move: Migration, immigration, emigration, and mobility (pp. 241-255). New York: Haworth.

Kozmetsky, R., & Kozmetsky, G. (1981). Making it together: A survival manual for the executive family. New York: The Free Press.

Krigsman, N., & Krigsman, R. (1988). How to successfully move an organization. Personnel Journal(January), pp. 65-72.

Kroger, J. E. (1980). Residential mobility and self concept in adolescence. Adolescence, 15(60), pp. 967-977.

Krupp, G. R., & Kligfeld, B. (1961, March). The bereavement reaction: A cross cultural evaluation. Digest of paper presented at the Thirty Eighth Annual Meeting of The American Orthopsychiatric Association, Statler Hilton Hotel, New York, p. 27.

Kübler-Ross, E. (1970). On death and dying. New York: First Collier.

Kunisch, R. D. (1980). Relocation in an unsettled economy. Personnel Administrator, 25(9), pp. 25-28.

Labor Letter-A special news report on people and their jobs in offices, fields, and factories. (1976, August 3). Wall Street Journal, p. 1.

Lacey, C., & Blane, D. (1979). Geographic mobility and school attainment: The confounding variables. Educational Research, 21(3), pp. 200-206.

Ladinsky, J. (1967). Occupational determinants of geographic mobility among professional workers. American Sociological Review, 32(2), pp. 257-264.

Ladinsky, J. (1967). The geographic mobility of professional and technical manpower. The Journal of Human Resources, 2(4), pp. 475-494.

Landis, J., & Stoetger, L. (1966). Migrant families: An explorative study of middle class migrant families. Journal of Marriage and the Family, 28, pp. 51-53.

Lang, D. V. (1988). The phantom spouse. New York: Dodd, Mead.

Lanier, A. R. (1979). Selecting and preparing personnel for overseas transfers. Personnel Journal, 58(3), pp. 160-163.

Lansing, J. D. (1966). Residential location and urban mobility. Ann Arbor: Institute for Social Research.

Larson, V. (1986, March-April). Relocating and family counseling: Formula to reduce stress and increase success. Mobility, pp. 57-60.

Laslett, B. (1971). Mobility and work satisfaction: A discussion of the use and interpretation of mobility models. American Journal of Sociology, 77(1), pp. 19-35.

Layton, A. (1987, May-June). Tearing down the barriers that create relocation reluctance. Mobility, pp. 73-74.

Lazarus, R. S. (1984). The costs and benefits of denial. In B. S. Dohrenwend & B. P. Dohrenwend (Eds.), Stressful life events & their contexts (pp. 131-155). New Brunswick: Rutgers University Press.

Le Louarn, J. Y., & DeCotis, T. A. (1983). The effect of working couple status on the decision to offer geographic transfer. Human Relations, 36(11), pp. 1031-1043.

LeCompte, M. D., Millroy, W. L., & Preissle, J. (1992). The handbook of qualitative research in education. San Diego: Academic.

Lee, E. S. (1966). A theory of migration, Demography (pp. 47-57). Chicago: Population Association of America.

Lefcourt, H. M. (1984). Locus of control and stressful life events. In B. S. Dohrenwend & B. P. Dohrenwend (Eds.), Stressful life events & their contexts (pp. 157-165). New Brunswick: Rutgers University Press.

Lehr, C. J., & Hendrickson, N. (1968). Childrens' attitudes toward a family move. Mental Hygiene, 52, pp. 381-385.

Leslie, G. R., & Richardson, A. H. (1961). Life-cycle, career pattern and the decision to move. American Sociological Review, 26(6), pp. 894-902.

Leslie, L. A. (1993). Families fleeing war: The case of central Americans, Marriage and Family Review (Vol. 19, pp. 193-205). New York: Haworth.

Leslie, L. A., & Grady, K. (1985). Changes in mothers' social networks and social support following divorce. Journal of Marriage and the Family, 47(3), pp. 663-673.

Levenson, M. K., & Hollmann, R. W. (1980). Personal support services in corporate relocation programs. Personnel Administrator, 25(9), pp. 45-51.

Levenstien, R. A. (1990, March). Why corporate transferees can't always make the best decisions for themselves. Mobility, pp. 49-50, p. 52, p. 54.

Levin, S. S., Groves, A. C., & Lurie, J. D. (1980). Sharing the move--Support groups for relocated women. Social Work(July), pp. 323-325.

Levine, M. (1966). Residential change and school adjustment. Community Mental Health Journal, 2(1), pp. 61-68.

Levine, S., & Scotch, N. A. (1970). Social stress. Chicago: Aldine.

Lewis, R. E. (1986). How to solve the problems encountered in group moves. Personnel Journal(January), p. 86, p.88, pp. 90-91.

Li, W. L. (1976). A note on migration and employment, Demography (pp. 565-570). Chicago: Population Association of America.

Lin, N., Dean, A., & Ensel, W. M. (1981). Social support scales: Metholodogical notes. Schizophrenia Bulletin, 7, pp. 73-87.

Lichter, D. T. (1980). Household migration and the labor market position of married women. Social Science Research, 9, pp. 83-97.

Lichter, D. T. (1982). The migration of dual-worker families: Does the wife's job matter? Social Science Quarterly, 63(1), pp. 48-57.

Lichter, D. T. (1983). Socioeconomic returns to migration among married women. Social Forces, 62(2), pp. 487-503.

Lidz, T. (1963). The family and human adaptation: Three lectures. New York: International Universities.

Liem, R., & Liem, J. H. (1984). Relations among social class, life events, and mental illness: A comment on findings and methods. In B. S. Dohrenwend & B. P. Dohrenwend (Eds.), Stressful life events & their contexts (pp. 234-255). New Brunswick: Rutgers University Press.

Lindemann, E. (1961, March). Dynamics of bereavement. Digest of paper presented at the Thirty Eighth Annual Meeting of The American Orthopsychiatric Association, Statler Hilton Hotel, New York, p. 28.

Lindenberger, T. J. (1987, March-April). The family in transition. Mobility, pp. 37-38.

Litwak, E. (1960). Geographic mobility and extended family cohesion. American Sociological Review, 25(3), pp. 385-394.

Litwak, E. (1960). Occupational mobility and extended family cohesion. American Sociological Review, 25(1), pp. 9-20.

Livermore, J. (1961, March). Some identification problems in adopted children. Digest of paper presented at the Thirty Eighth Annual Meeting of The American Orthopsychiatric Association, Statler Hilton Hotel, New York, p. 24.

Long, L. (1990). International perspectives on the residential mobility of America's children. Journal of Marriage and the Family, 54(4), pp. 861-869.

Long, L. H. (1970). On measuring geographic mobility. Journal of the American Statistical Association, 65(331), pp. 1195-1203.

Long, L. H. (1972). The influence of number and ages of children on residential mobility. Demography, 9(3), pp. 371-382.

Long, L. H. (1973). Migration differentials by education and occupation: Trends and variations. Demography, 10(2), pp. 243-258.

Long, L. H. (1974). Women's labor force participation and the residential mobility of families. Social Forces, 52(3), pp. 342-348.

Long, L. H. (1975). Does migration interfere with children's progress in school? Sociology of Education, 48(3), pp. 369-381.

Loomis, C. J. (1992). Spouses' reactions to employee relocation. (Doctoral dissertation, Northern Illinois University). University Microfilms International, No. 9313254 (1995).

Lord, V. M. (1987, July-August). Relocation: A family affair. Mobility, pp. 7-8.

Loth, B. (1990, July). I'm moving: Handle with care. Mobility, pp. 55-56.

Lubin, J. S. (1993, April 13). Husbands in limbo: As more men become 'trailing spouses,' firms help them cope. The Wall Street Journal, p. 1.

Lundy, M. (1994). Family relocation/family systems: Gender and the role of EAP. Employee Assistance Quarterly, 9, pp. 99-112.

Maccoby, M. (1976.. The corporate climber has to find his heart. Fortune,94, pp. 98-101,p. 104, p. 106, p. 108.

Macintosh, H. (1968). Separation problems in military wives. American Journal of Psychiatry, 125(2), pp. 260-265.

Mack, J. G. (1980). How companies can handle the complexities of relocation. Personnel Administrator, 25(9), pp. 59-61.

Macke, A. S. (1979). Housewives' self-esteem and their husbands' success: The myth of vicarious involvement. Journal of Marriage and the Family, 41(1), pp. 51-58.

Magnus, M., & Dodd, J. (1981). Relocation: Changing attitudes and company policies. Personnel Journal(July), pp. 538-548.

Mainker, M. C. (1982, January-February). Spouse career counseling. Mobility, pp. 29-30.

Managers move more but enjoy it less. (1976, August 23). Business Week, pp. 19-20.

Mann, P. A. (1972). Residential mobility as an adaptive experience. Journal of Consulting and Clinical Psychology, 39(1), pp. 37-42.

Marchant, K. H., & Medway, F. J. (1987). Adjustment and achievement associated with mobility in military families. Psychology in the Schools, 24(3), pp. 289-294.

Margolis, D. R. (1979). The managers. New York: William Morrow.

Markham, W. T., Macken, P. O., Bonjean, C. M., & Corder, J. (1983). A note on sex, geographic mobility, and career advancement. Social Forces, 61(4), pp. 1138-1146.

Marks, C. C. (1993). The bone and sinew of race: Black women, domestic service and labor migration. In B. H. Settles, D. E. Hanks III, & M. B. Sussman (Eds.), Families on the move: Migration, immigration, emigration, and mobility (pp. 149-173). New York: Haworth.

Marshall, C., & Rossman, G. B. (1976). Designing qualitative research. Newbury Park, California: Sage.

Marshall, J., & Cooper, G. L. (1976). The mobile manager and his wife, Management decision: Quarterly review of management technology (pp. 180-224). London, United Kingdom: Chemical & Marine Press.

Marsico, T., & Puskar, K. R. (1986). Family relocation: Helping children adjust. Pediatric Nursing, 12(2), pp. 108-110.

Marston, R. C. (1979). Orientation of international expatriates for Middle East assignments. Personnel Administrator, 24(8), pp. 21-26.

Martin, W. T. (1956). The structuring of social relationships engendered by suburban residence. American Sociological Review, 21(4), pp. 446-449.

Matter, D. E., & Matter, R. M. (1988). The stress of relocation: Action steps for the counselor. Elementary School Guidance & Counseling, 23, pp. 23-29.

Matthews, K. A., & Glass, D. C. (1984). Type A behavior, stressful life events, and coronary heart disease. In B. S. Dohrenwend & B. P. Dohrenwend (Eds.), Stressful life events & their contexts (pp. 167-185). New Brunswick: Rutgers University Press.

Maynard, C. E., & Zawacki, R. A. (1979). Mobility and the dual-career couple. Personnel Journal, 58(7), pp. 468-472.

McAllister, R. J., Butler, E. W., & Kaiser, E. J. (1973). The adaptation of women to residential mobility. Journal of Marriage and the Family, 35, pp. 197-204.

McAllister, R. J., Butler, E. W., & Kaiser, E. J. (1973). The consequence of feminine mobility. Personnel Administrator, 18(1), pp. 36-39.

McAuley, W. J., & Nutty, C. L. (1985). Residential satisfaction, community integration, and risk across the family life cycle. Journal of Marriage and the Family(February), pp. 125-130.

McBride, A. B. (1990). Mental health effects of women's multiple roles. American Psychologist, 45(3), pp. 381-383.

McCollum, A. T. (1990). The trauma of moving. Newbury Park, California: Sage.

McCollum, A. T., Jensen, N., & Copans, S. (1995, September). The shadowy side of moving. Mobility, pp. 33-37.

McCubbin, H. I., & Boss, P. G. (1980). Family stress and coping: Targets for theory, research, counseling, and education. Family Relations(October), pp. 429-430.

McCubbin, H. I., Boss, P. G., Wilson, L. R., & Lester, G. R. (Eds.). (1980). Developing family invulnerability to stress: Coping patterns and strategies wives employ in managing family separations. Stallhagsgatan, Sweden: International Library.

McCubbin, H. I., Dahl, B. B., Lester, G. R., Benson, D., & Robertson, M. L. (1976). Coping repertoires of families adapting to prolonged war induced separations. Journal of Marriage and the Family, 38, pp. 461-471.

McCubbin, H. I., Dahl, B. B., Lester, G. R., & Ross, B. A. (1975). The returned prisoners of war: Factors in family reintegration. Journal of Marriage and the Family(August), pp. 471-478.

McCubbin, H. I., Joy, C. B., Cauble, A. E., Comeau, J. K., Patterson, J. M., & Needle, R. H. (1980). Family stress and coping: A decade review. Journal of Marriage and the Family(November), pp. 855-871.

McCubbin, H. I., & Patterson, J. M. (1983). The family stress process: The double ABCX model of adjustment and adaptation. In H. I. McCubbin, M. B. Sussman, & J. M. Patterson (Eds.), Social stress and the family (pp. 7-37). New York: Haworth.

McCubbin, H. I., & Patterson, J. M. (1983). Family transitions: Adaptions to stress. In H. I. McCubbin, & C. Figley (Eds.), Stress and the family (pp. 5-25). New York: Bruner/Mazel.

McCubbin, H. I., & Thompson, A. I. (1991). Family assessment inventories for research and practice. Madison, Wisconsin: University of Wisconsin Press.

McKain, J. L. (1973). Relocation in the Military: Alienation and family problems. Journal of Marriage and the Family(May), pp. 205-209.

McKinney, J. (1986, November-December). Relocation counseling, key to easing transferee trauma. Mobility, pp. 49-50.

McMahon, T. (1988, Spring Conference Issue). Managing the personal and family impact of employee relocation. Mobility, pp. 83-86.

Meltzer, G., & Grandjean, E. (1989). The moving experience: A practical guide to psychological survival. Philadelphia: Multilingual Matters Ltd.

Mettelman, B. B. (1993). Exploring the process of adjustment to corporate relocation: The application of the cognitive appraisal model. (Doctoral dissertation Syracuse University). University Microfilms International No. 9409037 (1995).

Mezey, A. G. (1960). Psychiatric aspects of human migrations. International Journal of Social Psychiatry, 5(4), pp. 245-260.

Michelson, W. (1977). Environmental choice, human behavior and residential satisfaction. New York: Oxford University Press.

Michelson, W., Belgue, D., & Stewart, J. (1973). Intentions and expectations in differential residential selection. Journal of Marriage and the Family, May, pp. 189-196.

Milbrandt, G. F. (1981). Relocation strategies: Part I. Personnel Journal, 60(7), pp. 551-554.

Milbrandt, G. F. (1981). Relocation strategies: Part II. Personnel Journal, 60(8), pp. 644-646.

Miller, B. C., & Sollie, D. L. (1980). Normal stresses during the transition to parenthood. Family Relations(October), pp. 459-465.

Miller, C. R., & Butler, E. W. (1966). Anomia and eunomia: A methodological evaluation of Srole's anomia scale. American Sociological Review, 31(3), pp. 400-406.

Miller, S. W. (1971). A comment: The future of social mobility studies. American Journal of Sociology, 77(1), pp. 62-65.

Minuchin, S., & Nichols, M. P. (1993). Family healing. New York: The Free Press.

Mitchell, C. (1973). The age of transience. Personnel Administrator, 18(1), pp. 23-24.

Mitchell, E. D. (1980, May-June). Society in motion – a look at the 80's. Mobility, pp. 35-36.

Mobile society puts down roots. (1978, June 12). Time, pp. 73-74.

Monaghan, W. F., Sr. (1983, November-December). Profiling the relocated child. Mobility, pp. 57-58.

Morris, E. W., & Winter, M. (1975). A theory of family housing adjustment. Journal of Marriage and the Family, 37(1), pp. 79-88.

Morris, J. L., Pestaner, M., & Nelson, A. (1967). Mobility and achievement. Journal of Experimental Education, 35(4), pp. 74-80.

Morris, R. N. (1963). The assimilation of strangers in a small residential community. The Sociological Review, 11(1), pp. 5-17.

Morrison, A. M. (1980, June 16). The going gets lusher for employees that move. Fortune, pp. 159-160, p. 162, p. 164, p. 168, p. 173.

Moving on up. (1996, June 17). Newsbreak, 3(25), (www.relojournal.com.).

Mullen, E. (1989, March). Addressing the needs of the relocating child. Mobility, pp. 21-22.

Murino, C. (1989). Travelers come home to temporary housing. Personnel Journal(June), pp. 140-143.

Murray, J. D. (1990, May). Communication: A tool to guide transferees. Mobility, pp. 46-47, p. 49.

NEA Staff. (1958). America on the move. NEA Research Bulletin, 36(4), pp. 99-102.

Neims, M. R. (1986). The effects of relocation on the accompanying spouse in dual-career couples. (Doctoral dissertation, University of Florida). University Microfilms International No. 8618662 (1996).

Nelkin, D. (1972, April). Invisible migrant workers. Society, pp. 36-41.

Nemec, M. M. (1980). Today's relocation programs require greater sophistication and effective management. Personnel Administrator, 25(9), p. 22.

Neugebauer, R. (1984). The reliability of life-event reports. In B. S. Dohrenwend & B. P. Dohrenwend (Eds.), Stressful life events & their contexts (pp. 85-107). New Brunswick: Rutgers University Press.

Neumerski, J. (1994, April). A child's journey. Mobility, pp. 26-27.

Newman, S. J., & Owen, M. S. (1982). Residential displacement: Extent, nature, and effects. Journal of Social Issues, 38(3), pp. 135-148.

Nicco, D. (1995, December). The spouse comes first. Mobility, pp. 49-50.

Nicols, M. P., & Schwartz, R. C. (1991). Family therapy. Boston: Allyn & Bacon.

Nida, P. C., & Heller, W. M. (1987). The teenager's survival guide to moving. New York: Collier.

Oglesby, M. (1985). Relocation stress: An exploration of life changes, health and personality in the relocation process. (Doctoral dissertation, The University of Texas, Austin). University Microfilms International, No. 8609403 (1996).

Olive, L. E., Kelsey, J. E., Visser, M. J., & Daly, R. T. (1976). Moving as perceived by executives and their families. Journal of Occupational Medicine, 18, pp. 547-556.

Olkowski, T. T., & Parker, L. (1993). Moving with children: A parent's guide to moving with children. Littleton, Colorado: Gylantic.

Olson, S. K., & Brown, S. L. (1986). A relocation support group for women in transition. Journal of Counseling and development, 64, pp. 454-455.

Outland, J. (1992, January). Nothing to kid about: Relocating children is serious business. Mobility, pp. 51-52.

Packard, V. (1972). A nation of strangers. New York: David McKay.

Pahl, J. M., & Pahl, R. E. (1971). Managers and their wives. London: Allen Laine.

Panagos, J. L., Holmes, R. L., Thurman, R. L., Yard, G. J., & Spaner, S. D. (1981). Operation sail: One effective model for the assimilation of new students into a school district. Urban Education, 15(4), pp. 451-468.

Park, R. E. (1928). Human migration and the marginal man. American Journal of Sociology, 33(6), pp. 881-893.

Patton, M. Q. (1980). Qualitative evaluation methods. Beverly Hills, California: Sage.

Pedersen, F. A., & Sullivan, E. J. (1964). Relationships among geographic mobility, parental attitudes and emotional disturbances in children. American Journal of Orthopsychiatry, 34(3), pp. 575-580.

Peterson, E. P. (1994.. When families relocate. Homes Today,1, pp. 1-3.

Petrou, N. V. (1980, November-December). Employee relocation and productivity. Mobility, pp. 63-65.

Pfau, R. F. (1990). An analysis of the impact of programs designed to assist transferring students to adapt to a new school environment. (Doctoral dissertation, The Pennsylvania State University). University Microfilms International No. 9032362 (1996).

Phillips, E. L., Shenker, S., & Revitz, P. (1951). The assimilation of a new child into the group, Psychiatry (Vol. 14, pp. 319-325). New York: Guilford Press.

Phillips, S. L., & Fischer, C. S. (1984). Measuring social support networks in general populations. In B. S. Dohrenwend & B. P. Dohrenwend (Eds.), Stressful life events & their contexts (pp. 223-233). New Brunswick: Rutgers University Press.

Pierpoline, B. (1988, September-October). You can't go home again. Mobility, pp. 13-14.

Pierson, G. W. (1973). The moving American. New York: Alfred Knopf.

Pinder, C. C. (1979). Corporate transfer policy: Comparative reaction of managers and their spouses. Industrial Relations Industrielles, 33, pp. 654-664.

Pinder, C. C. (1989). The dark side of executive relocation. Organizational Dynamics, 17, pp. 48-58.

Piotrkowski, C. S. (1979). Work and the family system. New York: The Free Press.

Pogalies, J. L. (1973). Mobility: A way of life. Personnel Administrator, 18(1), p. 17.

Poloma, M. M., & Garland, T. N. (1971). The married professional woman: A study in tolerance of domestication. Journal of Marriage and the Family, 33(3), pp. 531-540.

Porter, O. L., & Rand, M. M. (1992). From here to there!: The workbook for families on the move. Portland: Niche.

Potter, C. J. (1964, December). Supervisory transfers: Opportunities unlimited. Supervision,26, pp. 4-6.

Pullen, C. (1990, October). There's no place like home: Is there? Mobility, pp. 43-44, p. 46, pp. 49-52.

Puskar, K. R. (1986). The usefulness of Mahler's phases of the separation-individuation process in providing a theoretical framework for understanding relocation. Maternal-Child Nursing, 15, pp. 15-22.

Puskar, K. R., & Caffo, S. M. (1986, January-February). Relocation: A corporate/employee balancing act. Mobility, pp. 45-47.

Rabkin, J. G., & Struening, E. L. (1976). Life events, stress, and illness. Science, 194, pp. 1013-1020.

Rackley, E. M. (1986, January-February). Relocating the mobile manager. Mobility, p. 53.

Rahe, R. H. (1984). Developments in life change measurement: Subjective life change unit scaling. In B. S. Dohrenwend & B. P. Dohrenwend (Eds.), Stressful life events & their contexts (pp. 49-62). New Brunswick: Rutgers University Press.

Ramey, L., & Cloud, J. C. (1987). Relocation success: A model for mental health counselors. Journal of Mental Health Counseling, 9(3), pp. 150-161.

Rapoport, R., & Rapoport, R. N. (1969). The dual-career family: A variant pattern and social change. Human Relations, 22(1), pp. 3-30.

Rapoport, R., & Rapoport, R. N. (1971). Further considerations on the dual career family. Human Relations, 24(6), pp. 519-533.

Rapoport, R., Rapoport, R. N., & Bumpstead, J. M. (Eds.). (1978). Working couples. New York: Harper Colophon.

Rapoport, R. N., & Rapoport, R. (1978). Dual-career families: Progress and prospects. Marriage and Family Review, 1(5), pp. 1-12.

Raymond, R., Jr., & Eliot, S. (1981). Five steps to set employee relocations on the right track. Personnel Administrator, 26(11), pp. 43-47.

Raymond, R. J., Jr., & Eliot, S. V. (1980, July-August). Employee relocation attitudes: The challenge of the 80's. Mobility, pp. 61-63.

Regan, M. C., & Roland, H. E. (1985). Rearranging family and career priorities: Professional women and men of the eighties. Journal of Marriage and the Family, 47, pp. 985-992.

Reibstein, L. (1992, January 20). Where the jobs are. Newsweek, pp. 42-44.

Renshaw, J. R. (1976). An exploration of the dynamics of the overlapping worlds of work and family. Family Process, 15(1), pp. 143-165.

Reynolds, C., & Bennett, R. (1991). The career couple challenge. Personnel Journal(March), pp. 46-48.

Reynolds, C., & Bennett, R. (1995). The career couple challenge (Adapted from March 1991 article). Personnel Journal(September Supplement), pp. 4-7.

Rhea, C. (1984, January-February). How to survive a move: Advice from the experts. Mobility, pp. 43-47.

Rich, K. (1989, November). Summers are for fun not for moving. Mobility, p. 55, pp. 57-58.

Richards, S., Donohue, K. C., & Gullotta, T. P. (1985). Corporate families and mobility: A review of the literature. Family Therapy, 12(1), pp. 59-71.

Richmond, A. H., & Lauga, A. C. (1961, March). Some observations concerning the role of children in the disruption of family homeostasis. Digest of paper presented at the Thirty Eighth Annual Meeting of The American Orthopsychiatric Association, Statler Hilton Hotel, New York, p. 29.

Rivlin, L. G. (1982). Group membership and place meanings in an urban neighborhood. Journal of Social Issues, 38(3), pp. 75-93.

Robbins, T. D. (1992). Maintaining marital unity in a mobile society: The effects of trailing spouse job assistance on dual-career couples. (Doctoral dissertation, Florida State University). University Microfilms International No. 9234246 (1995).

Roberts, B. O. (1987, Fall Workshop Issue). Business America: On the move. Mobility, pp. 70-71, pp. 73-75.

Robinson, B. E. (1982). Family experts on television talk shows: Facts, values, and half-truths. Family Relations, 31, pp. 369-378.

Robinson, T. (1981, May-June). The development of relocation assistance. Mobility, p. 69, p. 72, pp. 73-74.

Roman, B. D. (1992). Moving minus mishaps. Bethlehem, Pennsylvania: BR Anchor.

Romano, J. (1996, June 9). On moving day, some employers pitch in less. The New York Times, p. F10.

Rosenfeld, C., & Perrella, V. C. (1965). Why women start and stop working: A study in mobility, Monthly Labor Review (Vol. 88, pp. 1077-1082). Washington, D.C.: U.S. Department of Labor, Bureau of Labor Statistics.

Rosenman, R. H., Brand, R. J., Jenkins, C. D., Friedman, M., Straus, R., & Wurm, M. (1975). Coronary heart disease in the Western collaborative group study: Final follow-up experience of eight and one-half years. Journal of the American Medical Association, 233, pp. 872-877.

Rossi, P. H. (1955). Why families move. Glencoe, Illinois: The Free Press.

Rossi, P. H., & Schlay, A. B. (1982). Residential mobility and public policy issues: "Why families move" revisited. Journal of Social Issues, 38(3), pp. 21-34.

Sabagh, G., Van Arsdol Jr., M. D., & Butler, E. W. (1969). Some determinants of intrametropolitan residential mobility: Conceptual considerations. Social Forces, 48(1), pp. 88 97.

Sanders, D. (1984). Geographical mobility: A study of its relationship to self-concept and locus of control. Unpublished doctoral dissertation, University of Akron.

Scanzoni, J. (1981, August). Family: Crisis or change? Christian Century, pp. 794-799.

Schaller, J. (1975). The relation between geographic mobility and school behavior. Man-Environment Systems, 5(3), pp. 185-187.

Schetky, D. H. (1982). Corporate family lifestyles: A child psychiatrist's perspective. Psychiatric Annals, 12(9), p. 863, pp. 866-871.

Schlottmann, A. M., & Herzog Jr., H. W. (1984). Career and geographic mobility interactions: Implications for the age selectivity of migration. Journal of Human Resources, 19(1), pp. 72-86.

Schoeni, E. (1991, January-February). The relocation blues. EAP Digest, pp. 34-38, pp. 62-66.

Schorr, P. (1975). Planned relocation. Lexington, Massachusetts: D.C. Heath.

Schultz, C. (1986, July-August). The trailing spouse: The unsung hero. Mobility, pp. 84-85.

Schwartz, M. D. (1974). Situation/transition groups: A conceptualization and review. American Journal of Orthopsychiatry, 45(5), pp. 744-754.

Scudder, R., & Anderson, C. A. (1954). Migration and vertical occupational mobility. American Sociological Review, 19(3), pp. 329-334.

Seidenberg, R. (1973). Corporate wives - corporate casualties. New York: AMACOM.

Sekaran, U. (1986). Dual career families. Unpublished doctoral dissertation, University of Rochester, Rochester.

Sell, R. R. (1982). A research note on the demography of occupational relations. Social Forces, 60, pp. 859-865.

Settles, B. H. (1993). The illusion of stability in family life: The reality of change and mobility. In B. H. Settles, D. E. Hanks III, & M. B. Sussman (Eds.), Families on the move: Migration, immigration, emigration, and mobility (pp. 5-29). New York: Haworth.

Settles, B. H., Hanks III, D. E., & Sussman, M. B. (1993). Families on the move: Migration, immigration, emigration, and mobility. New York: Haworth.

Shaklee, H. (1989). Geographic mobility and the two-earner couple: Expected costs of a family move. Journal of Applied Social Psychology, 19(9), pp. 728-743.

Shahnasarian, M. (1989, September). A look at the psychology of the relocated spouse. Mobility, pp. 55-58.

Shamir, B., & Arthur, M. B. (1989). An exploratory study of perceived career change and job attitudes among job changers. Journal of Applied Social Psychology, 19(9), pp. 701-716.

Shaw, J. A. (1979). Adolescents in the mobile military community. Adolescent Psychiatry, 7, pp. 191-198.

Shaw, J. A., & Pangman, J. (1975). Geographic mobility and the military child. Military Medicine, 140, pp. 413-416.

Shrout, P. E. (1984). Conceptualization and measurement of stressful life events. In B. S. Dohrenwend & B. P. Dohrenwend (Eds.), Stressful life events & their contexts (pp. 28-47). New Brunswick: Rutgers University Press.

Shumaker, S. A., & Stokols, D. (1982). Residential mobility as a social issue and research topic. Journal of Social Issues, 38(3), pp. 1-20.

Sieveking, N., Anchor, K., & Marston, R. C. (1981). Selecting and preparing expatriate employees. Personnel Journal, 60(3), p. 197.

Sieveking, N. A., & Marston, R. C. (1978). Critical selection and orientation of expatriates. Personnel Administrator, 23(4), pp. 20-21.

Simonetti, J. L., Nykodym, N., & Goralske, J. M. (1988). Family ties: A guide for HR managers. Personnel, 65(1), pp. 37-41.

Simpson, G. A., & Fowler, M. G. (1994). Geographic mobility and children's emotional/behavioral adjustment and school functioning. Pediatrics, 93(2), pp. 303-309.

Simpson, M. E. (1970). Social mobility, normlessness, and powerlessness in two cultural contexts. American Sociological Review, 35(6), pp. 1002-1013.

Singer, M. (1982). Things that work: Moving groups. The School Counselor, 29(5), pp. 416-417.

Sirota, D., & Wolfson, A. D. (1973). Can employees be retrained, relocated? Personnel Administrator(January-February), pp. 33-35.

Skinner, D. A. (1980). Dual-career family stress and coping: A literature review. Family Relations(October), pp. 473-481.

Skinner, M. P. (1985, January-February). Attacking relocation stress: Southern Bell's answer. Mobility, pp. 80-81.

Skolnick, A., & Skolnick, J. (1992). Family in transition. In F. Walsh (Ed.), Normal family processes (2nd ed., p. 13). New York: Guilford.

Sluzki, C. E. (1979). Migration and family conflict. Family Process, 18(4), pp. 379-390.

Smardo, F. A. (1981). A selected bibliography/books about moving. Childhood Education, 58, pp. 37-42.

Smith, M. (1943). Some relationships between intelligence and geographic mobility. American Sociological Review, 8(1-6), pp. 657-665.

Solomon, C. M. (1996). One assignment, two lives. Personnel Journal(May), pp. 36-47.

Solomon, G. (1993, July). Are you ready for the stress of a relocation? National Business Employment Weekly, p. 22-24.

Soltis, J. F. (1990). The ethics of qualitative research. New York: Teachers College.

Sorokin, P. A. (1959). Social and cultural mobility. New York: The Free Press of Glencoe.

Spanier, G. B. (1985). Improve, refine, recast, expand, clarify – Don't abandon. Journal of Marriage and the Family, November, pp. 1073-1074.

Splete, H., & Rasmussen, J. (1977). Aiding the mobile child. Elementary School Guidance and Counseling, 2(3), pp. 225-228.

Sporakowski, M. J. (1993). Immigrant and migrant families: Issues in education and intervention. In B. H. Settles, D. E. Hanks III, & M. B. Sussman (Eds.), Families on the move: Migration, immigration, emigration, and mobility (pp. 299-310). New York: Haworth.

Springen, K., & Miller, A. (1989, July 3). Easing the moving blues. Newsweek, pp. 40-41.

Srole, L. (1956). Social integration and certain corollaries: An exploratory study. American Sociological Review, 21(6), pp. 709-716.

Srole, L. J. (1956). Anomie, authoritarianism and prejudice. American Journal of Sociology, 60(July), pp. 63-67.

Starker, J. E. (1988). The development of a social network following geographic relocation. (Doctoral dissertation, Portland State University). University Microfilms International No. 8813114 (1995).

Stautberg, S. S. (1988, May-June). relocation and the family. Mobility, pp. 41-46.

Stokols, D., & Shumaker, S. A. (1982). The psychological context of residential mobility and well being. Journal of Social Issues, 38(3), pp. 149-171.

Stouffer, S. A., & Lazarsfeld, P. E. (1972). Research memorandum on the family in depression. New York: Arno.

Strauss, N. (1981, November-December). The dual career phenomenon: Is it a threat to corporate relocation? Mobility, pp. 34-35.

Stroh, L. K. (1989). Corporate mobility: The effects on the children. Unpublished doctoral dissertation, Northwestern University, Evanston.

Stroh, L. K. (1993, December). Should teenage children in the home alter your mobility decision? Mobility, pp. 46-47, p. 49.

Stroh, L. K., & Brett, J. M. (1989, February). Corporate mobility: How do the children fare in the shuffle? Mobility, pp. 4-6, p. 9.

Stubblefield, R. l. (1955). Children's emotional problems aggravated by family moves. American Journal of Orthopsychiatry, 25, pp. 120-126.

Stuckert, R. P. (1963). occupational mobility and family relationships. Social Forces, 41(March), pp. 301-307.

Subota, N. (1986). Migration as one of the main causes of the weak adaptation of the family. Contemporary Family Therapy, 8(4), pp. 328-333.

Sussman, M. B. (1959). The isolated nuclear family: Fact or fiction. Social Problems, 6(4), pp. 333-339.

Sussman, M. B., & Burchinal, L. (1962). Kin family network: Unheralded structure in current conceptualization. Marriage and Family Living, 24(2), pp. 231-240.

Sussman, M. B., & Cogswell, B. E. (1971). Family influences on job movement. Human Relations, 24(6), pp. 477-487.

Sussman, M. B., & Settles, B. H., (1993). Policy and research issues regarding family mobility and immigration. In B. H. Settles, D. E. Hanks III, & M. B. Sussman (Eds.), Families on the move: Migration, immigration, emigration, and mobility (pp. 209-232). New York: Haworth.

Sutherland, A. (1972, January-February). Gypsies, the hidden Americans. Society, pp. 27-33.

Swenson, E. J. (1958). Transplanting children. NEA Journal, 47(5), pp. 332-334.

Switzer, R. E., Hirschberg, J. C., Myers, L., Gray, E., Evers, N. H., & Forman, R. (1961). The effect of family moves on children. Mental Hygiene, 45(4), pp. 528-536.

Syme, S. L., Borhani, N. O., & Buechley, R. W. (1965). Cultural mobility and coronary heart disease in an urban area. American Journal of Epidemiology, 82, pp. 334-346.

Syme, S. L., Hyman, M. M., & Enterline, P. E. (1965). Cultural mobility and the occurrence of coronary heart disease. Journal of Health and Human Behavior, 6, pp. 178-189.

Tausky, C., & Dubin, R. (1965). Career anchorage: Managerial mobility motivations. American Sociological Review, 30(10), pp. 725-735.

The case against executive mobility. (1972, October 28). Business Week, p. 110, p. 114.

The family move – Its psychological effects on children. (1970, February 13-14). From a symposium on "The effects of change of environment on the child" co-sponsored by Loyola University, Chicago and Allied Van Lines, The Guidance Center, Loyola University, Chicago.

Thomas, K. (Producer). (1997). The GI bill [Film]. WNET, N.Y.: Odyssey Films

Thomas, L. E., McCabe, E., & Berry, J. E. (1980). Unemployment and family stress: A reassessment. Family Relations, 29, pp. 517-524.

Thomas, W., & Znaniecki, F. (1927). The Polish peasant in Europe and America. New York: Knopf.

Thompson, E. (1980). The value of unemployment to the mothers of young children. Journal of Marriage and the Family(August), pp. 551-566.

Tiger, L. (1974, September). Is this trip necessary? The heavy human costs of moving executives around. Fortune, pp. 139-141, p. 182.

Todd, V. F. (1994). Who needs curtains anyway?: The impact of corporate relocation on the self concept of trailing wives. (Doctoral dissertation, University of Rochester). University Microfilms International No. 9509957 (1994).

Toffler, A. (1971). Future shock. New York: Bantam.

Toffler, A. (1980). The third wave. New York: Bantam.

Toliver, S. D. (1993). Movers and shakers: Black families and corporate relocation. In B. H. Settles, D. E. Hanks III, & M. B. Sussman (Eds.), Families on the move: Migration, immigration, emigration, and mobility (pp. 113-130). New York: Haworth.

Toney, M. B. (1976). Length of residence, social ties, and economic opportunities. Demography, 13(3), pp. 297-310.

Tönnies, F. (1957). Community & Society (Gemeinschaft und Gesellschaft) (Charles P. Loomis, Trans.). East Lansing: Michigan State University Press.

Tooley, K. (1970). The role of geographic mobility in some adjustment problems of children and families. Journal of the American Academy of Child Psychiatry, 9, pp. 366-378.

Torres, J. (1983, January-February). Facilitating family adjustment: A new technique. Mobility, pp. 71-72.

Transplanting the executive family. (1976, November 15). Business Week, pp. 159-161, p. 164, p. 166, p. 170.

Treder, D. J. (1991, December). Do we know which direction we're going? Mobility, pp. 49-51.

Trost, J. E. (1985). Abandon adjustment! Journal of Marriage and the Family, 47(November), pp. 1072-1073.

Tucker, E. (1990, March 12). A longing to go home. Time, p. 51.

Turner, C. (1971). Dual work households and marital dissolution. Human Relations, 24(6), pp. 535-548.

Upson, N. (1974). How to survive as a corporate wife. Garden City, New York: Doubleday.

Van Buren, M. (1984, May-June). Off-hour orientation programs: Using media to help transferees adjust to their new community. Mobility, p. 67, pp. 69-70.

Vandervelde, M. (1979). The changing life of the corporate wife. New York: Mecox.

Vecsey, G. (1975, November 7). More executives refusing to relocate. New York Times, p. 1, p. 15.

Veiga, J. F. (1973, January-February). The mobile manager at mid-career. Harvard Business Review, pp. 115-119.

Veiga, J. F. (1981, March-April). Do managers on the move get anywhere? Harvard Business Review, pp. 20-22, p. 26, p. 28, p. 30, p. 34, p. 36, p. 38.

Viney, L. A., & Bazeley, P. (1977). The affective reactions of housewives to community relocation. Journal of Community Psychiatry, 5, pp. 37-45.

Voles, L. A. (1982, May-June). Relocation through a child's eyes. Mobility, pp. 73-75.

Vorwaller, D. J. (1970). Social mobility and membership in voluntary associations. American Journal of Sociology, 75(4), pp. 481-495.

Voydanoff, P. (1980). Work roles as stressors in corporate families. Family Relations(October), pp. 489-494.

Walczak, J. (1985, January-February). Three keys to a successful move. Mobility, pp. 77-78.

Walker, K. N., MacBride, A., & Vachon, M. L. S. (1977). Social support networks and the crisis of bereavement. Social Science and Medicine, 11, pp. 35-41.

Wallston, B. S., Foster, M. A., & Berger, M. (1978). I will follow him: Myth, reality, or forced choice–Job seeking experiences of dual-career couples. In J. B. Bryson & R. Bryson (Eds.), Dual-career couples (pp. 9-21). New York: Human Sciences Press.

Walsh, F. (1993). Normal family processes. (2nd ed.). New York: Guilford.

Wamboldt, F. S., Steinglass, P., & De-Nour, A. K. (1991). Coping within couples: Adjustment two years after forced geographic relocation. Family Process, 30(November), pp. 347-361.

Watts, G. W. (1985, March-April). Dealing with the difficult transferee. Mobility, p. 75, pp. 77-78.

Wayman, P. H. (1990, May). On-site relocation centers: An alternative for meeting transferee needs. Mobility, pp. 57-58, pp. 60-61.

Weinhaus, E. (1996, May). Those difficult transferees. Mobility, pp. 63-64.

Weiss, R. S. (1969). The fund of sociability. Trans-Action, 6, pp. 36-43.

Weiss, R. S. (1973). The experience of emotional and social isolation. Cambridge, Massachusetts: The MIT Press.

Weissman, M. M., & Paykel, E. S. (1972, July-August). Moving and depression in women. Society,9, pp. 24-28.

Werbel, J. D. (1983). Job change: A study of an acute job stressor. Journal of Vocational Behavior, 23, pp. 242-250.

Werkman, S. L. (1979). Introduction: The effects of geographic mobility on adolescents. Adolescent Psychiatry, 7, pp. 175-177.

Westoff, C. F., Bressler, M., & Sage, P. C. (1960). The concept of social mobility: An empirical enquiry. American Sociological Review, 25(3), pp. 375-384.

Whalen, T. E., & Fried, M. A. (1973). Geographic mobility and its effect on student achievement. Journal of Educational Research, 67(4), pp. 163-166.

Why moving day comes less often now for executives. (1975, January 13). U.S. News & World Report, p. 51, p. 53.

Whyte, W. H., Jr. (1951, October). The wives of management. Fortune, pp. 86-88, p. 201, p. 202, pp. 206-208, p. 210, p. 213.

Whyte, W. H., Jr. (1953, May). The transients. Fortune, pp. 112-117, p. 221, p. 222, p. 224, p. 226.

Whyte, W. H., Jr. (1953, June). The future, c/o Park Forest. Fortune, pp. 126-132, p. 188, p. 190, p. 192, p. 194, p. 196.

Whyte, W. H., Jr. (1953, July). The outgoing life. Fortune, pp. 84-88, pp. 156-159.

Whyte, W. H., Jr. (1953, August). How the new suburbia socializes. Fortune, pp. 120-122, p. 186, pp. 188-190.

Whyte, W. H., Jr. (1956). The organization man. Garden City, New York: Doubleday Anchor Books.

Wilson, C. (1994, January). Relocation from the transferee's perspective. Mobility, pp. 40-43.

Wilson, C. (1994, February). Children–The full circle. Mobility, pp. 103-105.

Wilson, C. M. (1985, July-August). Dual career families: Issue of the 80's. Mobility, pp. 93-95.

Wilson, C. M. (1988, May-June). Employee relocation: A reflective perspective. Mobility, p. 34, p. 36, p. 38.

Wilson, C. M. (1989, August). Inside relocation. Mobility, pp. 71-74.

Wilson, C. M. (1990, September). The changing work force: Still mobile? Mobility, pp. 33-36, pp. 38-39.

Winfield, F. E. (1986). The changing face of corporate relocation. Personnel, 63(1), pp. 33-40.

Winkelman, M. (1994). Cultural shock and adaptation. Journal of Counseling and Development, 73, pp. 121-126.

Wolcott, H. F. (1992). Posturing in qualitative inquiry. In M. D. LeCompte, Millroy, W. L., & Preissle, J. Eds. (Ed.), The handbook of qualitative research (pp. 3-44). San Diego: Academic.

Wood, D., Halfon, N., Scarlata, D., Newacheck, P., & Nessim, S. (1993). Impact of family relocation on children's growth, development, school function and behavior. Journal of the American Medical Association, 270(September 15), pp. 1334-1338.

Wood, H. C. (1958). Children who move with the crops. NEA Journal, 47(3), pp. 170-172.

Worthington, E., Jr. (1987). Treatment of families during life transitions: Matching treatment to family response. Family Process, 26(June), pp. 295 -308.

Yee, W., & Van Ardsdol, M. D., Jr. (1977). Residential mobility, age, and the life cycle. Journal of Gerontology, 32(2), pp. 211-221.

Young, W. D. (1989, June). Questions and answers about moving with children. Mobility, pp. 46-47, p. 49, p. 51.

Young, W. D. (1990, April). Relocation stress: Myth or reality. Mobility, pp. 27-30.

Young, W. D. (1990, May). Relocation 2001. Mobility, pp. 63-64, pp. 66-68.

Ziller, R. C., & Behringer, R. D. (1961). A longitudinal study of the assimilation of the new child into the group. Human Relations, 14(2), pp. 121-134.

Ziller, R. C., Behringer, R. D., & Jansen, M. J. (1961). The newcomer in open and closed groups. Journal of Applied Psychology, 45(1), pp. 55-58.

Zippo, M. (1980). Employee relocation: It's a whole new ballgame. Personnel(March-April), pp. 70-73.

Zunker, V. G. (1990). Career counseling: Applied concepts of life planning. Pacific Grove, California: Brooks/Cole.

Zutler, S. H. (1983, March-April). The five stages of relocation stress and how to cope. Mobility, pp. 70-71.

BIOGRAPHY OF THE AUTHOR

Barbara Watts Cummings was born in the Bronx, New York in 1940. She received a Bachelor of Science in Education (1962) from Fordham University, married that same year, and began life as a corporate wife. She raised their two children, Tracy and Sean, in fourteen different locations including two overseas assignments. During an eight year stay in Belgium she was President of the American Women's Club of Brussels, an overseas organization of 1000+ members, whose primary goal was to help corporate wives adjust to living in a foreign culture. This began her interest in working with relocating families and upon returning to the United States she entered graduate school at St. Louis University and received a Master of Arts in Counseling (1993). She began working as a consultant for a local St. Louis relocation company. She has been active as a teacher, counselor, and community volunteer and upon completion of her Ph.D. plans to work as an independent consultant for relocating corporate families. She and her husband Michael live in St. Louis, Missouri and she refuses to move.

CPSIA information can be obtained
at www.ICGtesting.com
Printed in the USA
BVHW03s0213090718
521151BV00001B/34/P

9 781581 120530